D0921260

MIDDLE EASTERN
MYTHOLOGY

MIDDLE EASTERN MYTHOLOGY

S. H. HOOKE

DOVER PUBLICATIONS, INC.
MINEOLA, NEW YORK

Copyright

Copyright © 1963 by S. H. Hooke

Bibliographical Note

This Dover edition, first published in 2004, is an unabridged republication of *Middle Eastern Mythology: From the Assyrians to the Hebrews,* published by Penguin Books, New York, 1963.

Library of Congress Cataloging-in-Publication Data

Hooke, S. H. (Samuel Henry), 1874-1968.
Middle Eastern Mythology / S. H. Hooke.
    p. cm.
    Originally published: New York : Penguin Books, 1963, in series: Pelican books.
    Includes bibliographical references and index.
    ISBN 0-486-43551-2 (pbk.)
    1. Mythology, Middle Eastern. I. Title.

BL1060.H66 2004
201'.3'09394—dc22

        2004043931

Manufactured in the United States of America
Dover Publications, Inc., 31 East 2nd Street, Mineola, N.Y. 11501

CONTENTS

5

Contents

LIST OF PLATES

7

PREFACE

THE purpose of this book is to give some account of the mythology of the ancient Near East. During the last fifty years the labours of archaeologists have revealed the rich stores of documents, tablets, and inscriptions buried in the ruined sites of the ancient cities of Egypt, Sumer, Assyria, Babylonia, Asia Minor, and Syria. The decipherment and translation of cuneiform and Hittite texts have made available to students a new and surprising amount of mythological material, throwing fresh light on the whole field of myth. An attempt is here made to describe and give examples of this new material. We have also ventured to offer a classification of myths from the functional point of view. A discussion of the place of myth in Christianity has been included in this study because of its direct connexion with the use of myth in the religion of Israel.

Acknowledgements are due to the Princeton University Press for permission to quote from Professor J. R. Pritchard's *Ancient Near Eastern Texts relating to the Old Testament*; also to the Falcon's Wing Press, Colorado, for permission to quote from Professor Noah Kramer's book, *From the Tablets of Sumer*; also to the Clarendon Press for permission to use material from my book *In the Beginning*, and from *Myth and Ritual*. The footnotes will indicate my indebtedness to many other authors and sources. I have to thank my wife for careful revision of the MS.

INTRODUCTION

SINCE there is a considerable amount of ambiguity in the meaning and use of the term 'myth', it is desirable that something should be said about its use in this book. The usual distinction drawn between myth, legend, saga, folk-story, and *Märchen* is based upon literary criteria; a further current usage distinguishes between myth and historical truth, with the implication that anything which is characterized as a myth is unworthy of belief. The criterion used in this study is neither literary, nor historical, but functional. The myth is a product of human imagination arising out of a definite situation and intended to do something. Hence the right question to ask about the myth is not, 'Is it true?' but 'What is it intended to do?'

In studying the very varied mythological material yielded by the ancient Near East, and using the notion of 'function' as a criterion, it is possible to distinguish the following types of myth:

TYPES OF MYTH

The Ritual Myth

It is a well-established fact that most of the texts from which our knowledge of the myths here described is taken have been found in temple archives. They imply the existence in the river-valleys of the Nile and the Tigris–Euphrates of a highly developed urban civilization resting on an agricultural basis. These texts show that the dwellers in Egypt and Mesopotamia had created an elaborate pattern of activities, to which we give the name of *ritual*. These activities were carried on by large staffs of priests in the temples. They constituted a system of actions performed in a fixed way, at regular times, by authorized persons who possessed the specialized knowledge of the correct way in which these actions should be carried out. The whole elaborate pattern of activities was designed to secure the well-being of the community by controlling the incalculable forces by which man found himself surrounded. But we now know that the ritual did not consist only of actions; the actions were accompanied by spoken words, chants, and incantations, whose magical efficacy was an essential part of the ritual. In other words, the ritual consisted of the part which was *done*, which the Greeks called the *drōmenòn*, and the *spoken* part, which they called the *muthos*, or *myth*. In the ritual the myth told the story of what was being enacted; it described a situation; but the story was not told to amuse an audience; it was a word of power. The repetition of the magic words had power to bring about, or recreate, the situation which they described. We shall see later that, at a central point in the Babylonian New Year Festival, the priests recited the chant called *Enuma elish*, which was the myth of Creation; and the recitation *did* something; it brought about a change in the situation which the ritual was enacting.

Thus we may understand that in a society where such rituals formed an essential part of the life of the community, the historical truth of the story contained in the myth was irrelevant. The function of history is to find out and to record as accurately as possible the behaviour of communities in the past, i.e., to discover and impart a certain kind of knowledge. The function of the myth was not knowledge but action, action essential for the very existence of the community. Mankind has in the past existed for vast periods of time without feeling any need for history; but, long before the appearance of the earliest forms of historical records, the myth had a vital function in the life of the community; as an essential part of ritual it helped to secure those conditions upon which the life of the community depended. This is why we have called this type of myth the *ritual myth*. It takes its name from its function, which is to aid in securing the efficacy of the ritual. It is possible that this was the earliest type of myth to come into existence.

The Myth of Origin

This type of myth is more generally called the *aetiological myth*. This myth is also very early; some scholars would regard it as the earliest. Its function is to give an imaginary explanation of the origin of a custom, a name, or even an object. For example, we shall see that the Sumerian myth of Enlil and the Pickaxe is a story intended to explain how that most valuable agricultural implement came into existence through the activity of a god. Another example is the Hebrew myth of Jacob's conflict with a supernatural being. This story offers an explanation of an ancient Israelite food-tabu.

The Cult Myth

In the development of the religion of Israel a new use of myth makes its appearance. The three seasonal festivals prescribed in the *Book of the Covenant* were celebrated at the various local shrines, such as Bethel, Shechem, and Shiloh, during the early stages of Israel's settlement in Canaan. Offerings were brought, and each of the festivals, Passover, Pentecost or the Feast of Weeks, and Tabernacles, had its own special ritual, preserved and carried out by the priests at the local shrines. On these occasions an important part of the ritual consisted in the public recitation by the priests of certain central events in the history of Israel; the recitation was accompanied by antiphonal responses from the people. One of the most deeply rooted traditions of Israel was that of the deliverance of the people from Egyptian bondage. At the Feast of Passover this event was celebrated with a ritual whose origin was far older than the historical event thus commemorated. Accompanying the ritual was the cult myth describing the event, not in historical terms, but in terms borrowed in part from Babylonian and Canaanite myth. The function of the cult myth was to confirm the covenant relation between Yahweh and Israel, and to magnify the power and glory of Yahweh. In this new use of the myth it was divested of the magical potency which it had possessed in the ritual myth. We can see the cult myth still further developed in the prophetic use of it as a means of presenting the conception of 'salvation-history' to Israel. The myth still describes a situation, and still has the function of securing the continuance of the situation, no longer by magical, but by moral force. The function of the myth has been lifted to a higher plane in the cult myth as we see it employed by the prophets of Israel.

The Prestige Myth

There is a form of the myth, distinct from any of the foregoing, which calls for notice. Its function is to invest the birth and exploits of a popular hero with an aura of mystery and wonder. While the story of the birth and exposure of Moses in an ark of bulrushes on the Nile may rest upon historical tradition, it can be paralleled by similar stories relating to Sargon, Cyrus, Romulus and Remus, and other heroes of popular imagination. The birth and exploits of the Danite hero, Samson, are related in mythical terms intended to glorify the tribe of Dan and its hero. It may be remarked in passing that the attempt to find a sun-myth in the story of Samson is generally discredited. The stories of the exploits of Elijah and Elisha fall into the same category, although in this case the motive of magnifying the glory of Yahweh is also present. Prestige myths also tend to gather round the names of famous cities. Troy is built by the hands of gods, and even Zion is described in mythical terms borrowed from Babylonian and Canaanite mythology as being built 'on the sides of the north', the expression used in those myths to describe the abode of the gods.

The Eschatological Myth

Although it may owe something to the eschatology of Zoroastrianism, the eschatological myth is specially characteristic of Jewish and Christian thought. In the writings of the prophets, and above all in the apocalyptic literature, the conception of a catastrophic end of the present world-order has a prominent place. The prophets believed that the 'salvation-history' must have its consummation in a decisive divine intervention. 'It shall come to pass in the last days' is a characteristic phrase in the prophetic vocabulary. When the prophets attempt to describe the final situation they have to fall back on the language of myth. The description of the conquest of the chaos-dragon by Marduk in the Babylonian Epic of Creation supplies them with the imagery which they use to describe Yahweh's final victory over the forces of evil. Just as the divine act of creation lies outside the horizon of history and can only be described in the language of myth, so the divine act that brings history to a close can only be described in the same terms. The eschatological use of myth was carried over from

Judaism into Christianity and appears in its fullest display in the Apocalypse of St John.

It may, perhaps, be necessary to say that the application of the category of myth to the Gospel narratives is in no way intended to call in question their essential historical veracity. But for those who believe, as the prophets of Israel and the first disciples of Jesus did, that God has entered into human history, there are certain moments in history when events take place whose causes and nature lie beyond the range of historical causation. Here the function of myth is to express in symbolical terms, by means of images, what cannot be otherwise put into human speech. Here myth has become an expansion of symbolism.

THE DIFFUSION AND DISINTEGRATION
OF MYTHS

There are two ways in which the presence of myths in any society may be explained; one is by way of diffusion, and the other is through the independent working of imagination when confronted by similar situations. Usener's researches have shown that the myth of the Flood is to be found in almost every part of the world. We shall see when we come to deal with the Sumerian and Babylonian forms of the Flood myth that its presence in the region of the Tigris–Euphrates valley can be explained as due to the periodical occurrence there of disastrous floods. But when we find the Flood myth in countries where such floods are not possible, as in Greece or Canaan, for instance, it becomes clear that the myth has been brought there from the place of its origin, even if it is no longer possible to trace the method of diffusion. An example of the way in which myths might travel from their source is furnished by the discovery in Egypt of a cuneiform tablet containing the Babylonian myth of Adapa, with which we shall deal later. The tablet had been used by Egyptian scribes for the purpose of learning cuneiform. A similar instance occurred when a fragment of the myth of Gilgamesh was discovered during the American excavation of Megiddo. The legend of Cadmus tells us how the Phoenician alphabet was carried to Greece and became the parent of all our Western alphabets. Thus there are reasonable grounds for assuming that travel, trade movements, migrations of peoples, and invasions were a means of diffusion by which myths might be carried from one country to another.

It can be observed that rituals decayed and disappeared, or were transformed with the decay of the civilization in which they had played such an important part. Then we find that the myths attached to the decaying rituals were freed from their ritual associations and became literary forms, passing into the traditions of other peoples. For example, the myth of the slaying of the dragon which is, as we shall see, a central element in the Babylonian myth of Creation has given birth to the legends of Perseus and Andromeda, Hercules and the Lernaean Hydra, Siegfried and Fafnir, Beowulf and Grendel, and still survives in the mummers' play of St George and the Dragon.

Chapter 1

MESOPOTAMIAN MYTHS

BEFORE we begin to give an account of the most important myths which have their origin in Mesopotamia, something should be said about the early cultural conditions out of which the myths which we are to examine came into existence in that part of the ancient Near East. Archaeological excavation of the sites of the ancient cities in the Tigris–Euphrates valley has shown that this region, known as Sumer and Akkad, was inhabited as early as 4000 B.C. by a people known as the Sumerians. Some scholars are of the opinion that there are traces of an earlier settlement, but it is certain that the fully developed civilization revealed by excavation of such sites as Ur, Erech, and Kish was the work of the Sumerians. They appear to have come into the delta from the mountainous region to the north-east of Mesopotamia, and their myths show that they came from a very different kind of country from that which they found in their new home. The form of writing called cuneiform was their invention, and it was they who built the strange temple-towers known as 'ziqqurats' which are such a characteristic feature of their cities. Their language was of the type known as agglutinative, and its linguistic affiliations are uncertain. Their remains, as illustrated, for example, by Sir Leonard Woolley's excavation of Ur, show a highly developed civilization of an agricultural type, with splendid temples, priests, laws, literature, and a rich mythology. At an early date, but probably later than the Sumerian settlement of the delta of the Tigris–Euphrates, the first wave of Semitic invasion entered the region of Sumer and Akkad, gradually conquered the Sumerians, absorbed their culture, and adopted their cuneiform script, but not their language. The language of the Semitic invaders is known as Akkadian, and is one of the important branches of the great Semitic family of languages of which Arabic is the ancestor. The second wave of Semitic invasion by a people known as Amurru, or Amorites, resulted in the foundation of the first Amorite dynasty in Babylon, and the rise of Babylon under Hammurabi to the hegemony of Sumer and Akkad. The date of the first king of the Amorite dynasty has been assigned to about 2200 B.C. About 500 years later another Semitic people who had settled higher up the Tigris valley, between the upper and lower Zab, conquered Babylon and established the first Assyrian empire in Mesopotamia. Hence the mythology of Mesopotamia has come to us in Sumerian, Babylonian, and Assyrian forms, and while there is little difference between the Babylonian and Assyrian forms of any particular myth, there are very considerable differences between, for example, the Sumerian and the Assyro–Babylonian form of the Creation myth. Moreover, some curious Sumerian myths have no Semitic counterpart. We shall begin our account of Mesopotamian mythology with the Sumerian material.

SUMERIAN MYTHS

Among the great mass of mythological material which is now available through the devoted labours of Sumerologists, three types of myth appear whose distribution is so widespread that they might justly be called *basic* myths. It is clear that, although these three basic myths appear in Semitic mythology, their origin is Sumerian, hence we shall begin our account of Sumerian myths with them.

Middle Eastern Mythology

The Myth of Dumuzi and Inanna

The first of these myths has long been known as the descent of Ishtar into the underworld and existed in a fragmentary form; but as the result of Professor Kramer's skilled labours it is now known in a complete form as the myth of Dumuzi and Inanna. Dumuzi is the Sumerian form of the more familiar name Tammuz, while Inanna is similarly the Sumerian equivalent of the Semitic Ishtar, the queen of heaven. Dumuzi is the prototype of all the vegetation gods who die and rise again with the rebirth of vegetation in the spring. In the form of the myth underlying the Tammuz liturgies, the imprisonment of the god in the underworld is a principal motive of the myth and is the cause of Inanna's descent into the underworld. But in the earliest form of the myth as given by Kramer in *The Ancient Near Eastern Texts relating to the Old Testament* the reason for the descent of the goddess is not given. The form of the myth here related follows Kramer's version.[1]

For reasons unknown, Inanna, the queen of heaven, decides to go down into the nether world, the 'land of no return', ruled over by her sister, the goddess Ereshkigal. Kramer suggests that the motive may have been ambition, the desire to bring the nether world under her dominion. To provide against any disasters that may happen to her in the nether world, Inanna instructs her vizier, Ninshubur, that if she does not return in three days he is to perform mourning rites for her, and to go in turn to the three high gods, Enlil of Nippur, Nanna the moon-god of Ur, and Enki, the Babylonian god of wisdom, in Eridu, and entreat them to intervene on her behalf that she may not be put to death in the nether world. Then Inanna puts on her queenly apparel and her jewels, and approaches the gate of the nether world. There she is challenged by Neti, the gate-keeper of the seven gates. By the orders of Ereshkigal and in accordance with the laws of the nether world, Inanna, as she passes through the seven gates, is stripped of an item of her apparel at each gate; she is brought before Ereshkigal and the Anunnaki, the seven judges of the nether world. They turn 'the eyes of death' upon her and she is turned into a corpse and hung upon a stake. After three days, as she does not return, Ninshubur does as he was directed by Inanna. Enlil and Nanna refuse to intervene, but Enki performs certain magical operations by which Inanna is restored to life. Out of dirt from his finger-nail he creates two strange creatures, the *kurgarru* and the *kalaturru*, the meaning of whose names is unknown, and sends them to the nether world with the food of life and the water of life. They are told to sprinkle the food of life and the water of life sixty times upon the corpse of Inanna. They do so and the goddess is restored to life. It is a law of the nether world that no one may return from thence without providing a substitute. Hence the myth goes on to describe the ascent of Inanna to the land of the living accompanied by demons who are to carry back to the nether world the substitute whom she provides. First Ninshubur, then Shara the god of Umma, and then Latarak the god of Badtibira are in turn claimed by the demons and rescued by Inanna. Here the text as given in *The Ancient Near Eastern Texts* breaks off, but Kramer adds in a footnote to his introductory summary of the myth a surprising addition recently discovered. According to this fragment of the myth, Inanna and her escort of demons come to her own city of Erech and there find her husband Dumuzi. He does not humble himself before her as the other three had done, and she therefore hands him over to the demons to be carried off to the nether world. Dumuzi entreats Utu, the sun-god, to deliver him, and here the fragment breaks off. Hence we do not know whether, in the original Sumerian form of the myth, Dumuzi, who is Tammuz, was carried away by the demons into the nether world.

This is the first of the three basic myths referred to above in its Sumerian form. It is possible that the Sumerians brought the myth with them when they settled in the delta, and that this is its earliest form. In this form Inanna does not descend into the nether world to bring back her husband/brother Dumuzi, or Tammuz, from death. On the contrary and against all later conceptions of the myth, it is Inanna who allows the demons to carry off Dumuzi to the nether world as her substitute, while the reason for her own descent is left unexplained. Nevertheless, the Tammuz-liturgies [2] which belong to the Sumerian period already show the later form of the myth. They describe the chaos and desolation which fall upon the land when Tammuz goes down into the nether world; they describe Ishtar's lamentation and her descent into the nether world to rescue Tammuz from its powers; and they conclude with a description of the triumphant return of Tammuz to the land of the living. It is also clear that the liturgies form part of a seasonal ritual, and hence that the myth may rightly be classed as a ritual myth. A possible reason for the change in the original form of the myth may be found in the fact that the Sumerians, in coming into the delta, were passing from a pastoral economy to an agricultural mode of life. In the liturgies Tammuz and Ishtar are frequently represented under the figure of the male and female fir-tree, and the fir-tree is not found in the Tigris–Euphrates delta, but belongs to the mountainous region from which the Sumerians came. Moreover, the fact that the towering 'ziqqurats' were a feature of Sumerian temple architecture has been held to point in the same direction. Hence the original form of the myth may have arisen under conditions of life which were very different from the agricultural mode of life which the Sumerians were obliged to adopt when they settled in the delta. There is evidence to show that Semites and Sumerians were both occupying the delta for a considerable time before the Amorite invasion and the final conquest and absorption of the Sumerians by the Semites. We know that the Semites took over from the Sumerians their cuneiform script and much of their religion and mythology, and this may well be accepted as a further explanation of the changed character of the Tammuz-Ishtar myth as we find it in the Assyro-Babylonian period. We shall see later what changes the myth underwent as it passed into other countries.

The Myth of Creation

The second basic myth which we find in a Sumerian form is the wide-spread myth of Creation. It may be remarked here that we do not find the conception of creation *ex nihilo* in any of the ancient myths of Creation. For all of these, creation is the act of bringing order out of an original state of chaos. When we come to deal with the Assyro–Babylonian material, we shall see that the cosmogonic myth existed there in one main form, the well-known Enuma Elish, or Epic of Creation, as it is now generally styled. But there is nothing corresponding to this in the Sumerian material. Professor Kramer has shown that Sumerian cosmogony has to be pieced together from various myths of origin, and the following account is based on his researches. He is, however, careful to remind us that there are great gaps in our knowledge of Sumerian, and that many of the tablets upon which the myths have been preserved are broken and incomplete. Hence, in the present state of our knowledge of Sumerian it is impossible to give a completely coherent account of Sumerian mythology.

For the sake of convenience the Sumerian myths of Creation may be arranged under three heads: the origin of the universe, the organization of the universe, and the creation of man.

The Origin of the Universe. In a tablet which contains a list of the Sumerian gods, the goddess Nammu, whose name is written with the ideogram for 'sea', is described as 'the mother who gave birth to heaven and earth'. From other myths it appears that heaven and earth were originally a mountain whose base was the earth and whose summit was heaven. Heaven was personified as the god An, and earth as the goddess Ki, and from their union was begotten the air-god Enlil, who then separated heaven from earth and brought the universe into being in the form of heaven and earth separated by air. Sumerian mythology gave no explanation of the origin of the primeval sea.

The Organization of the Universe. This aspect of the creation motif is dealt with in a number of myths which describe how the heavenly bodies and all the various elements of Sumerian civilization came into being. The first of these myths is concerned with the birth of the moon-god, Nanna, or Sin. The details are far from clear, and further knowledge may modify them; but the outline of the myth seems to be that Enlil, the high god of the Sumerian pantheon, whose shrine was at Nippur, was enamoured of the goddess Ninlil and raped her as she was sailing on the stream Nunbirdu. For this high-handed act Enlil was banished to the underworld, but Ninlil, great with child, refused to be left behind, and insisted on following Enlil to the nether world. As this would have involved the birth of Ninlil's child Nanna, the moon-god, in the dark nether world instead of becoming the light of the sky, Enlil devised a complicated scheme by which Ninlil became the mother of the three deities of the nether world as substitutes for Nanna, who was thus enabled to ascend to heaven. It is clear that this curious and hitherto unknown myth gives a clue to the transformation of the Tammuz–Ishtar myth, of which we have already spoken. We can see from the Tammuz liturgies that Enlil is a frequent title of Tammuz, and similarly that Ninlil is a frequent designation of Ishtar; so that the descent of Ishtar into the nether world, which, as we have seen, is unexplained in the earliest form of the Sumerian myth of Inanna's descent into the nether world, finds an explanation in this myth of the birth of Nanna, the moon-god.

In the Sumerian pantheon the moon-god, Nanna, or Sin, was the chief astral deity, and the sun-god, Utu, was regarded as the offspring of Nanna and his consort Ningal. In the later Hebrew cosmogony the position was reversed and the sun became the major luminary, while the moon became female, as in classical mythology. The Sumerians conceived of Nanna as journeying through the night sky in a *quffah*, the circular boat used in the navigation of the Euphrates, accompanied by the stars and planets, whose origin is not explained.

After Enlil had separated heaven from earth, and the illumination of heaven had been provided in the forms of Nanna, Utu, and the stars and planets, the organization of the earthly part of the universe had to be undertaken, and various myths deal with the different elements of the terrestrial order. It should be observed that, somewhat illogically, the cities and temples of the gods are thought of as existing before the creation of man, which comes at the end of the various divine activities involved in creating the order of the universe. Enlil is conceived of as the ultimate source of vegetation, cattle, agricultural implements, and

the arts of civilization, though he brings these into being
indirectly by the creation of lesser gods who carry out his
instructions. In order to provide cattle and grain for the
earth, at the suggestion of Enki, the Babylonian Ea, the god
of wisdom, Enlil creates two minor deities, Lahar, the cattle-
god, and Ashnan, the grain-goddess, to provide food and
clothes for the gods. The myth describes the abundance
which they create upon earth; but they drink wine and get
drunk and begin to quarrel, neglecting their duties, so that
the gods are unable to obtain what they need. In order to
remedy this situation man is created. The following is
Kramer's translation of part of the myth of Lahar and
Ashnan :

> In those days, in the creation chamber of the gods,
> In their house Dulkug, Lahar and Ashnan were fashioned;
> The produce of Lahar and Ashnan,
> The Anunnaki of the Dulkug eat, but remain unsated;
> In their pure sheepfolds milk, . . . and good things,
> The Anunnaki of the Dulkug drink, remain unsated;
> For the sake of the good things in their pure sheepfolds,
> Man was given breath.

In addition to myths relating to the provision of food and
clothing, there are various myths dealing with other elements of civilization and the organization of the universe.
A long poem, much of which is still obscure, describes the
creation of the pickaxe by Enlil and the gift of this valuable
implement to 'the black-headed people' to enable them to
build their houses and cities. Another myth describes the
activities of Enki in providing Sumer with the necessary
elements of civilization. The myth describes how Enki, beginning with Sumer, journeys through different parts of the
world, 'fixing the destinies', a Sumerian term meaning the
creative activity of the gods in bringing order into the
universe. First Enki visits Ur, then Meluhha, which might

possibly signify Egypt, then the rivers Tigris and Euphrates
which he fills with fishes, and then the Persian Gulf. Over
each of these he appoints a god or goddess to take charge.
A passage from Kramer's translation of this interesting myth
will illustrate the nature of Enki's civilizing activities:[3]

> The plough and the yoke he (Enki) directed,
> The great prince Enki caused the ox to . . .;
> To the pure crops he *roared*,
> In the steadfast field he made grain grow;
> The lord, the jewel and ornament of the plain,
> The . . . farmer of Enlil,
> Enkimdu, him of the canals and ditches,
> Enki placed in their charge.
> The lord called to the steadfast field, he caused it to produce
>   much grain,
> Enki made it bring forth its small and large beans . . .
> The . . . grains he heaped up for the granary,
> Enki added granary to granary,
> With Enlil he increases abundance in the land;
> Her whose head is . . . whose face is . . .
> The lady who . . . the might of the land, the steadfast support
>   of the black-headed people,
> Ashnan, strength of all things,
> Enki placed in charge.

Enki then goes on to place the brick-god, Kabta, in charge
of the pick-axe and the brick-mould. He lays foundations
and builds houses, and places them under the charge of
Mushdamma, the 'great builder of Enlil'. He fills the plain
with vegetable and animal life, and places Sumuqan, 'king
of the mountain', in charge. Lastly, Enki builds stables and
sheepfolds and places them under the shepherd-god Dumuzi.

The last myth dealing with the organization of the universe to which we shall refer is concerned with the activities of the goddess Inanna, or Ishtar. We have already had
occasion to refer to the expression 'fixing the destinies',

and we shall see when we come to deal with Babylonian myths that an object called 'the tablet of destinies' plays an important part in several myths. The possession of it was one of the attributes of deity, and we hear of the tablets being stolen or taken by force on several occasions. The god who possessed them had the power of controlling the order of the universe. In the myth with which we are now dealing, Inanna wishes to confer the blessings of civilization upon her own city, Erech. In order to do this she must acquire the *me*, a Sumerian word which appears to denote the same power as that which is conferred by the possession of the Akkadian 'tablets of destiny'. The *me* are in the hands of Enki, the god of wisdom. Accordingly, Inanna journeys to Eridu, where Enki dwells in his house of the Apsu, the sweet-water abyss. Enki receives his daughter Inanna hospitably and makes a great feast for her. When he gets merry with wine he promises her all kinds of gifts, including the *me*, or divine decrees which, in Kramer's words, are 'the basis of the culture pattern of Sumerian civilization'. The myth contains a list of over a hundred items which constitute the elements of Sumerian civilization. Inanna receives the gifts with joy, and loads them on her bark, 'the boat of heaven', and sets sail for Erech. When Enki recovers from his orgy he realizes that the *me* are missing from their accustomed place. The mention of a place in which the *me* are kept suggests that they are in the form of tablets. On discovering his loss Enki sends his messenger Isimud with instructions to recover them. Seven times he attempts to do so, but each time he is foiled by Ninshubur, Inanna's vizier, of whom we have already heard. So the goddess brings to Erech the blessings of civilization. It will be noted that the various myths to which we have referred reflect the rivalry which existed between the various city-states of Sumer. The first items on the list of the *me* which

Inanna obtained from Enki are those referring to lordship:
the crown, throne, and sceptre are mentioned, from which
we may infer that the struggle for the hegemony of Sumer
is one of the motives underlying these myths of the organ-
ization of the universe. *The Creation of Man.* We have already seen that the myth
of Lahar and Ashnan ended up with the creation of man
for the service of the gods.

Another myth, the text of which is difficult and broken,
describes the way in which man was created. Although the
Sumerian myth differs considerably from the account given
in the Babylonian Epic of Creation, both versions agree in
the object for which man was created, namely, for the service of the gods, to till the ground and free the gods from
having to work for their living. In the Sumerian myth the
gods complain that they cannot get their food. Enki, the
god of wisdom, to whom the gods generally resort in time
of need, is asleep; but Nammu, the primeval ocean, the
mother of the gods, arouses him from sleep. By Enki's instructions Nammu and Ninmah, the goddess of birth, assisted by deities, whom Kramer's rendering describes as
'good and princely fashioners', mix clay which is 'over the
abyss' and bring man into existence. The tablet is broken
and the text is difficult and obscure, but some curious details
emerge. Enki gives a banquet to the gods to celebrate the
creation of man. Enki and Ninmah drink much wine and
become drunk. Ninmah takes some of the clay which is
'over the abyss' and creates six different kinds of human
beings whose nature is obscure, except in the case of the
last two, which are the barren woman and the eunuch.
Enki decrees the fate of the eunuch as destined to stand before the king. The myth goes on to describe a further act
of creation by Enki. He creates a human being who is feeble
in mind and body, and then asks Ninmah to do something

to improve the condition of the miserable creature, but she is unable to do anything and curses Enki for making such a creature. One of the Hebrew words for man is *enosh*, a root one meaning of which is 'weak' or 'sick'. This aspect of humanity is often emphasized in Hebrew poetry, and this curious element in the Sumerian myth may possibly underlie the Hebrew representation of man as failing to measure up to the place in the universe which the divine purpose had intended for him. We shall see later that important differences appear in the Babylonian myth of Creation which are not without significance in their influence on the Hebrew account of how man was created.

The Myth of the Flood

The third of the basic myths is the wide-spread myth of the Deluge. Usener's well-known work has shown that the myth of the destruction of mankind by a flood is to be found in some form or other in every part of the world, as we have already seen (p. 16). The central motive of the myth is that the gods decide to destroy mankind; the means by which they do so is secondary, and we shall see that water is not the only means used. It has long been known that the Biblical story of the Deluge was based on the Babylonian myth which will be dealt with when we come to the next stage of our study. But that the Babylonian form of the myth was based on an earlier Sumerian version was not known until 1914, when the American scholar Arno Poebel published a fragment of a Sumerian tablet containing episodes of what was clearly the myth of the Flood. No further Sumerian tablets relating to the Flood have yet been discovered. The outlines of the Sumerian version of the Flood story are as follows. At the point where the fragment continues the story, a god appears to be declaring his intention of saving mankind from the destruction which the gods have decided to bring upon them. The reason for their decision is not given. Enki is the god who takes steps to save mankind from destruction. Apparently he instructs Ziusudra the pious king of Sippar to stand by a wall, through which he will reveal to Ziusudra the dire intention of the gods, and tell him what must be done to escape the coming flood. The part of the text which must have described the building of the boat is missing, but its existence is implied in the following passage which describes the Flood and Ziusudra's escape :

All the windstorms, exceedingly powerful, attacked as one,
At the same time, the flood sweeps *over the cult-centres.*
After, for seven days (and) seven nights,
The flood had *swept over* the land,
(And) the huge boat had been tossed about by the windstorms
     on the great waters,
Utu came forth, who sheds light on heaven (and) earth.
Ziusudra opened a *window of* the huge boat,
The hero Utu *brought his rays into* the giant boat.
Ziusudra, the king,
Prostrated himself before Utu,
The king kills an ox, *slaughters* a sheep.

Then, after a break, the tablet describes the ultimate fate of Ziusudra :

Ziusudra, the king,
Prostrated himself before Anu (and) Enlil.
Anu (and) Enlil cherished Ziusudra,
Life like (that of) a god they give him,
Breath eternal like (that of) a god they *bring down* for him.
Then, Ziusudra the king,
The *preserver of the name of vegetation (and)* of the seed of
     mankind,
In the land *of crossing,* the land of Dilmun, the place where
     the sun rises, they caused to dwell.[4]

Middle Eastern Mythology

It may be inferred from the Babylonian story of the Flood that the complete Sumerian version contained much fuller details about the cause of the flood and the building of the boat; but these may be left until we come to deal with the Akkadian mythology. The question whether the myth of the Flood, the third of our basic myths, can be classed with ritual myths, presents difficulties; but this, too, may be left until we have discussed the fuller form of the Flood myth, and its connexion with the Gilgamesh myth.

In addition to the three basic myths described above, there are a number of Sumerian myths which must be included in our account of what is perhaps, the oldest mythology in the world with the possible exception of the Egyptian one. It must also be borne in mind that our knowledge of Sumerian is still far from complete, and the meaning of many words in that language is uncertain; moreover, many of the tablets are in a fragmentary condition, and often extremely hard to read. Hence, while the account given here of the Sumerian myths rests upon the best contemporary scholarship, further research and fresh discoveries may well make changes and additions necessary in the future.

The Myth of Enki and Ninhursag

A myth which has no counterpart in Akkadian mythology, so far as our knowledge goes at present, and one which Kramer has described as one of the best preserved of the Sumerian myths, is the myth of Enki and Ninhursag. In *The Ancient Near Eastern Texts* it is described as a Paradise myth, and some of its features may underlie the Hebrew account of Paradise.

The outline of the myth is as follows: the scene is laid in Dilmun, described both as a land and a city, and identified by modern scholars with Bahrain in the Persian Gulf. The protagonists are the god Enki, the water-god, and the goddess Ninhursag, the earth-mother. The myth begins with a description of Dilmun as a clean, pure, bright place, where the animals do not harm one another, and where there is no sickness nor old age. The only thing wanting in Dilmun is sweet water, and this is provided by Enki at Ninhursag's request. The Myth then goes on to relate that from the union of Enki and Ninhursag is born Ninsar, or Ninmu, the goddess of plants. Ninhursag's period of gestation is described as lasting nine days, a day for each month of human gestation. Enki then impregnates his daughter Ninsar, who gives birth to the goddess Ninkurra, and she, in turn, being impregnated by Enki gives birth to the goddess Uttu, also described as the goddess of plants. Her name must not be confused with the name of the sun-god Utu. Then Ninhursag warns Uttu against Enki, and gives her certain advice as to how she is to deal with Enki's approaches. Following the advice Uttu demands a present of cucumbers, apples, and grapes, possibly as wedding gifts. Enki brings the required gifts and is joyfully received by Uttu; as the result of their union eight plants spring forth, but, before Ninhursag can assign them their names and qualities, Enki eats all the plants. Ninhursag, infuriated, curses Enki with a terrible curse and departs. The gods are dismayed, and Enki is stricken with sickness in eight different parts of his body. Through the craft of the fox, Ninhursag is induced to return and cure Enki of his sickness. She does this by creating in succession eight deities, one for each part of Enki's body in which the sickness is located. It has been pointed out that there is a punning relation between the name of each deity and the particular part of Enki's body affected. The closing lines of the poem seem to suggest that the eight deities are regarded as Enki's children, and their destiny is fixed by Ninhursag. This curious myth does not seem to have any counterpart in the field of Near Eastern mythology, except in so far as the concept of a golden age in the past is wide-spread, and the incestuous relation between father and daughter finds an echo in the relation between Saturn and Vesta in Greek mythology, as Milton's lines remind us:

> Thee bright-haired Vesta, long of yore
> To solitary Saturn bore;
> His daughter she, in Saturn's reign
> Such mixture was not deemed a stain.

But we have no clue to the interpretation of the details of the myth. Professor Thorkild Jacobsen has said with regard to it, 'This myth endeavours to trace a causal unity among many disparate phenomena, but it is a unity causal in the mythopoeic sense only. When plants are seen as born of soil and water, we can still follow, although with reservations. Towards the end of the myth, however, the deities born that Enki may be healed have no intrinsic connexion either with soil who bears them, or with water.' [5] The myth does at least show that although the Babylonians borrowed much from Sumerian mythology, the Semitic mind found it difficult to accept many elements in that mythology.

The Myth of Dumuzi and Enkimdu

Another Sumerian myth is of interest as finding an echo in the Hebrew story of Cain and Abel, but without its tragic ending. It deals with the age-long rivalry between the agricultural and the pastoral modes of life. In the myth Inanna, or Ishtar, is about to choose a husband. The choice lies between the shepherd-god Dumuzi, or Tammuz, and the farmer-god Enkimdu. Inanna's brother Utu, the sun-god, favours Dumuzi, but Inanna herself prefers Enkimdu. Dumuzi urges his suit and claims to have everything that Enkimdu can offer and more. Enkimdu endeavours to appease Dumuzi and offers him all kinds of gifts, but Dumuzi remains determined to have Inanna, and apparently succeeds in his intention, since, as we have already seen, various myths represent Dumuzi as the husband of Inanna. Kramer's rendering of the conclusion of the poem is worth quoting. Enkimdu speaks:

'Thou, O shepherd, why dost thou start a quarrel?
O Shepherd Dumuzi, why dost thou start a quarrel?
Me with thee, O shepherd, me with thee why does thou
    compare?
Let thy sheep eat the grass of the earth,
In my meadowland let thy sheep *pasture*,
In the fields of Zabalam let them eat grass,
Let *all* thy *folds* drink the water of my river Unun.'

Dumuzi speaks:

'I, the shepherd, at my marriage do not enter, O farmer, as my
    friend,
O farmer, Enkimdu, as my friend, O farmer, as my friend, do
    not enter.'

Enkimdu replies:

'Wheat I shall bring thee, beans I shall bring thee,
Beans of . . . I shall bring thee,
The maid Inanna (*and*) *whatever is pleasing* to thee,
The maid Inanna . . . I shall bring thee.'[6]

When we come to deal with Hebrew myths we shall see that various layers of older myths underlie the present form of the Cain and Abel myth, and it is possible that Dumuzi's rejection of all the farmer-god's gifts underlies Yahweh's rejection of Cain's agricultural offerings.

Gilgamesh Myths

An important figure in Akkadian mythology is the hero Gilgamesh, who is, according to the Gilgamesh Epic, two parts god, and one part man. But he also belongs to Sumerian mythology, and three Sumerian texts included in *The Ancient Near Eastern Texts* in Kramer's translation contain accounts of episodes in which Gilgamesh is concerned. It should be remarked here that in the Sumerian king-lists Gilgamesh is the fifth king of the dynasty of Erech, the second dynasty after the Flood according to Sumerian reckoning. The first of these texts, entitled 'Gilgamesh and Agga' in *The Ancient Near Eastern Texts*, reflects the struggles for domination between the early Sumerian city-states. It contains the story of the conflict between Gilgamesh of Erech and Agga the last king of the dynasty of Kish, the first dynasty after the Flood. Much of the poem is obscure, but it seems to represent a demand by Agga for the submission of Erech, the resistance of the demand by Gilgamesh, the siege of Erech by Agga, and a final reconciliation of the two kings. There is no intervention of the gods, hence the text is not strictly speaking part of Sumerian mythology, and is only included here because of its evidence that the figure of Gilgamesh is derived from Sumerian sources. The second text, entitled in *The Ancient Near Eastern Texts* 'Gilgamesh and the Land of the Living', clearly contains mythical material which was utilized in the composition of the Akkadian Epic of Gilgamesh, with which we shall deal later. Its theme is the search for immortality, a motive which underlies much of Near Eastern mythology. As the substance of this text has been taken up and more fully developed in the Akkadian Epic mentioned above, it need only be briefly summarized here. Oppressed by the all-pervasiveness of death, and conscious that he himself cannot escape it, Gilgamesh determines to find the Land of the Living. His friend and servant Enkidu, of whom we shall learn more in the Akkadian Epic, advises him to consult the sun-god Utu about his adventure. Utu at first warns him of its dangers, but afterwards helps him to cross the seven mountains and reach his goal which appears to be the cedar mountain where the giant Huwawa dwells. Gilgamesh and Enkidu, after some obscure preliminaries, cut off the giant's head. Here the tablet breaks off. The importance of the text lies chiefly in the fact that it shows the Sumerian preoccupation with the problem of death, and that it is the source from which the Babylonians drew the materials for the complete Gilgamesh story given in the Akkadian form of the myth.

The third Gilgamesh fragment, entitled in *The Ancient Near Eastern Texts* 'The Death of Gilgamesh', further develops the theme of death and the quest for immortality. Gilgamesh appears to have had a dream which is interpreted to him by the god Enlil as meaning that the gods have denied immortality to mankind, but that Gilgamesh has been granted fame, wealth, and success in battle. The second part of the poem appears to describe a funerary ritual, which may, as Kramer suggests, throw light on the significance of the death-chamber discovered by Sir Leonard Woolley in his excavation of Ur. The Sumerians may, like the ancient Egyptians, have immolated the wives and court attendants on the occasion of the death of a king; the text appears to imply that Gilgamesh has died, and ends with a paean in his praise.

Here we may leave the subject of Sumerian mythology, and pass on to the Akkadian, that is, the Assyro–Babylonian mythology, much of which is, as we have already pointed out, based on the Sumerian material. It must be borne in mind that the Semitic conquerors of the Sumerians, while they adopted the Sumerian cuneiform script, adapted it to express a Semitic language (Akkadian) totally unlike Sumerian. Hence many of the gods of the Sumerian pantheon adopted by the Babylonians and Assyrians appear under Semitic names in the Akkadian mythology. Inanna becomes Ishtar, Utu becomes Shamash, the moon-god Nanna becomes Sin, although many of the names of the temples and ritual terms retain their Sumerian forms. Many of the prayers and incantations continued to be recited by the priests in Sumerian, which remained the language of religious ritual and liturgy long after it had ceased to be a spoken language, much as Latin continued, and still continues, to be the liturgical language of the Church. The Akkadian forms of Sumerian myths thus reflect both the altered political conditions of Semitic domination, and the different mentality of the Semitic conquerors.

BABYLONIAN MYTHS

We have, for convenience, classed the myths described in this section as Babylonian, although many of the texts which contain them were written by Assyrian scribes and come from the library of the Assyrian king, Ashurbanipal. Professor Sidney Smith has said:[7] 'It is certain that the Assyrian scribes were engaged in transforming the literature they borrowed from Babylonia from the style of the First Dynasty of Babylon to the form in which we find it in Ashurbanipal's library.' All the gods of Assyria were also worshipped in Babylonia, and the Assyrian religious festivals were celebrated at the same times and in the same way as those of Babylonia. There are a few myths or legends peculiar to Assyria, such as the legend of Sargon of Agade, which has a very curious history. But in the main the myths which we shall describe are of Babylonian provenance, and represent the Semitic transformation of earlier Sumerian material.

We shall begin by giving the Babylonian form of the three basic or type myths already described in the previous section:

The Descent of Ishtar into the Nether World

As in the Sumerian version, so also in the Babylonian form of the myth, no reason is given for Ishtar's descent into the nether world; but at the end of the poem, after Ishtar has been released, Tammuz is introduced as Ishtar's brother and lover, without any explanation of how he comes to be in the nether world. The lines that follow seem to imply the return of Tammuz to the land of the living with rejoicings. It is only from the Tammuz liturgies that we learn of the imprisonment of Tammuz in the underworld, and of the desolation caused by his absence from the land of the living. In the Babylonian version of the descent of Ishtar to the land of no return, we have a description of the failure of all sexual fertility caused by her absence: 'the bull springs not upon the cow; the ass impregnates not the jenny; in the street the man impregnates not the maiden.' [8] It is with these words that Papsukkal, the vizier of the great gods, announces the non-return of Ishtar and its consequences. The description of the descent of the goddess follows the Sumerian version in its main outlines; but there are some interesting differences. When Ishtar knocks at the gate of the underworld she threatens to batter down the gate if she is not admitted, and to set free the dead who are in the underworld. A vivid passage of the poem describes this scene:

O gatekeeper, open thy gate,
Open thy gate that I may enter!
If thou openest not the gate so that I cannot enter,
I will smash the door, I will shatter the bolt,
I will smash the doorpost, I will move the doors,
I will raise up the dead, eating the living,
So that the dead will outnumber the living.[9]

Ishtar, in this version of the myth, is a much more hostile and threatening figure than she is in the Sumerian version. We also find in Ishtar's threat to let loose the dead upon the living an illustration of the Babylonian fear of ghosts which was such a marked feature of their religion and appears in so many of their incantations. As Ishtar passes through the seven gates she is stripped of some part of her apparel at each gate, as in the Sumerian version. The Babylonian version omits the grim description of her being turned into a corpse by the baleful 'eyes of death' however, she does not return, and then follows Papsukkal's appeal to the great gods quoted above. In answer to this appeal Ea, who is Enki in the Sumerian version, creates Asushunamir the eunuch, and sends him down to induce Ereshkigal to give him the life-water bag. By his charm he succeeds in doing this, and Ereshkigal reluctantly orders her vizier Namtar to sprinkle Ishtar with the water of life. Ishtar is released and returns, receiving back those articles of adornment and apparel which had been taken from her as she passes through the seven gates on her return journey. But a reference is made to the ransom which she must pay. Ereshkigal says to Namtar, 'If she does not give thee her ransom-price, bring her back.' What this is to be is not specified, but the mention of Tammuz at the end of the myth seems to imply his return from the underworld, although no indication has been given as to how he came there. We have already seen that there is a Sumerian myth of Enlil's

Mesopotamian Myths

banishment to the underworld and of Inanna's accompanying him there, and reference has been made to the identification of Tammuz with Enlil in the liturgies. Hence it would seem that in the course of the development of the myth the descent of Tammuz into the underworld came to assume increasing importance, and to be related to the death and rebirth of vegetation. When, in the course of time, the myth was carried into other countries, it was the death of Tammuz and the mourning for him that came to be emphasized at the expense of other features of the myth. Thus we have a reference in Ezekiel [10] to the women of Israel weeping for Tammuz, and the myth of Venus and Adonis represents the form in which the myth had passed into Greek mythology. Milton's reference to the river Adonis running 'purple to the sea, supposed with blood of Thammuz yearly wounded', is a reminder of the Syrian form of the myth, and we shall see that the death of Baal in the Ugaritic mythology may represent an earlier stage of the development of the myth in its passage to Syria.

The Creation Myth

We have seen that in the Sumerian version of the second basic myth, the myth of Creation, the creative activities are shared among various gods, Enlil and Enki being the principal figures concerned in creation. But in Babylonia the myth of Creation assumed central importance owing to the fact that it became associated with the great Babylonian New Year, or Akitu, Festival and was embodied in liturgical form in the poem or chant known from its opening words as *Enuma elish*, 'When on high'. In this form of the myth the Babylonian god Marduk plays the principal part. It is he who conquers Tiamat, secures the tablets of destiny, and performs the various creative acts described in the poem. The seven tablets containing the myth were first discovered by the British excavation of Nineveh, and parts of them were translated and published by George Smith in 1876. Over-hasty enthusiasts immediately made comparisons between the seven days of Creation in the Priestly account in Gen. 1 and the seven tablets of the Babylonian myth, and advanced the theory that the Hebrew form of the Creation story was entirely dependent on the Babylonian. We shall return to this point when we come to deal with Hebrew mythology. Since then, further portions of the tablets have been discovered and some of the gaps in the first discovery have been filled. Most modern scholars assign the date of the composition to the beginning of the second millennium B.C., the period when Babylon was becoming the leading city of the Akkadian city states. We know from such portions of the Babylonian New Year liturgy as remain to us that at two points of the New Year Festival ritual the priests recited the *Enuma elish* with the force of a magical incantation.

The German excavation of the site of Ashur, the old capital of the Assyrian empire, brought to light the Assyrian version of the *Enuma elish*, in which the name of the Babylonian god Marduk was replaced by the name of Ashur the chief god of Assyria.

The outline of the myth in its Babylonian form is as follows: Tablet one begins with a description of the primeval condition of the universe when nothing existed except Apsu, the sweet-water ocean, and Tiamat, the salt water ocean. From the union of these two the gods were brought into existence. The first pair, Lahmu and Lahamu (interpreted by Jacobsen [11] as the silt deposited at the junction of the sea and the rivers) gave birth to Anshar and Kishar, interpreted by the same scholar as the circular horizons of sky and earth. Anshar and Kishar in turn give

Mesopotamian Myths

birth to Anu, the sky, and Nudimmud or Ea, the earth- and water-god. Here a break with the Sumerian tradition appears. Enlil, whose activities we have already seen in the Sumerian mythology, is replaced by Ea, or Enki, who appears in Babylonian mythology as the god of wisdom and the source of all magic. Ea then begets Marduk, the hero of the Babylonian form of the myth. But before the birth of Marduk we have an account of the first conflict between the primeval gods and those whom they have begotten. Tiamat and Apsu are disturbed by the noise of the younger gods and take counsel with Mummu, Apsu's vizier, how to destroy them. Tiamat is reluctant to destroy her offspring, but Apsu and Mummu devise a plan. Their intention is disclosed to the gods who are alarmed, but Ea, the all-wise, devises a counter-scheme; he casts a spell of sleep upon Apsu, slays him, binds Mummu and puts a cord in his nose. He then builds his sacred chamber and calls it 'Apsu', and rests in profound peace. In this chamber the birth of Marduk takes place, and a description of his beauty and tremendous strength follows. The first tablet ends with a description of the preparation for a renewed conflict between the primeval gods and the younger gods. Tiamat is reproached by her other children for having remained quiescent when Apsu was destroyed, and they succeed in stirring her up to take measures for the annihilation of Anu and his associates. She makes Kingu, her firstborn, the leader of the attack, arms him, and invests him with the tablets of destiny. She then begets a horde of monstrous beings, such as the scorpion-man and the centaur whom we find depicted on Babylonian seals and boundary-stones. She places Kingu at the head of this host, and prepares to avenge Apsu.

The second tablet describes how the news of the coming attack is received by the assembly of the gods. Anshar is

43

troubled and smites his thigh in dismay. He first reminds Ea of his previous victory over Apsu and suggests that he should deal with Tiamat in the same way; but Ea either refuses to go or is unsuccessful; the text is broken at this point, and what happens to Ea is not clear. Then Anu is sent armed with the authority of the assembly of the gods to turn Tiamat from her purpose, but he also returns unsuccessful. Then Anshar rises in the assembly of the gods and proposes that Marduk, the strong hero, should be entrusted with the task. Marduk's father Ea advises him to accept the task, and Marduk agrees to undertake it on condition that he is given full and equal authority in the assembly of the gods, and that his word is to determine destiny unalterably. Here the second tablet ends.

The third tablet, after recapitulating the decision of the gods, ends with a feast at which Marduk is to be officially invested with the authority which he had demanded.

The fourth tablet begins with the enthronement of Marduk as king and his investment with the royal insignia. The gods require from him a proof that he possesses the power to carry out what he has undertaken. He thereupon causes his robe to disappear and then to reappear. The gods are satisfied and proclaim, 'Marduk is king.' Then Marduk arms himself for the combat; his weapons are bow and arrows, mace, lightning, and a net held at the corners by the four winds; he fills his body with flame, and creates the seven raging hurricanes; he mounts his storm-chariot, and advances against Tiamat and her host. He challenges Tiamat to single combat; he casts his net to enclose her, and when she opens her mouth to swallow him he drives in the evil wind to distend her and transfixes her with his arrow, splitting her heart. Her demon helpers flee, but are caught in the net and bound. Their leader, Kingu, also is caught and bound. Then Marduk takes from Kingu the tablets of destiny and fastens them upon his own breast, thus assuming supreme authority among the gods. His next act is to split the body of Tiamat in two; he places half of her above the earth as the sky, fixes it with bars, sets guards, and charges them not to let her waters escape. He then builds Esharra, the abode of the great gods, after the pattern of Ea's abode Apsu, and causes Anu, Enlil, and Ea to occupy their places therein. Here ends the fourth tablet.

The fifth tablet is too fragmentary to enable us to obtain from it a complete account of Marduk's first steps in organizing the universe, but its opening lines show that his first care was the calendar, one of the most important responsibilities of a Babylonian king. Marduk is represented as establishing the course of the year and the order of the months by the moon's changes. He also establishes the three celestial 'ways', the way of Enlil in the northern heavens, the way of Anu in the zenith, and the way of Ea in the south. The planet Jupiter is placed in charge of the heavenly order.

In the sixth tablet we have the description of the creation of man. Marduk declares his intention of creating man for the service of the gods. By the advice of Ea it is decided that the leader of the rebellion, Kingu, shall die that mankind may be fashioned. Accordingly Kingu is slain, and from his blood mankind is created for the service of the gods, 'to free them', that is, to perform the menial tasks belonging to the temple ritual and to provide food for the gods. Then the gods build a temple for Marduk, the great Esagila temple in Babylon with its ziqqurat. At the command of Anu they proclaim the fifty great names of Marduk, a proceeding which occupies the rest of the poem. This is the outline of the Babylonian myth of creation, and the underlying Sumerian elements can easily be detected. But the elements which were scattered over a number of Sumerian myths have, in the *Enuma elish*, been brought together and welded into a coherent whole. We have no evidence that the various Sumerian myths ever formed part of a ritual. They can be explained, as Professor Thorkild Jacobsen has so ably done, on aetiological lines. But while the aetiological factor is still discernible in *Enuma elish*, the poem has now become a ritual myth, possessing magical potency, and playing a vital part in the Babylonian New Year Festival in connexion with the dramatic representation of the death and resurrection of the god.

The Myth of the Flood

The third of our basic myths is the myth of the Flood. In this case the somewhat fragmentary Sumerian myth has been considerably expanded in its Babylonian form and has been embedded in the Gilgamesh Epic. We shall deal with the Babylonian form of the saga of Gilgamesh later, but the Flood myth is linked up with the Gilgamesh Epic so as to form part of the adventures of its hero.

A mythological theme almost entirely absent from Sumerian mythology so far as we know it at present, but very prominent in Semitic mythology, is the problem of the existence of death and sickness, and the quest for immortality. In the Gilgamesh Epic the problem is forced upon Gilgamesh by the death of his companion Enkidu, of whom we shall hear more when we deal with the other parts of the Epic; but at present we are concerned with the connexion between the Epic and the Flood myth. After the description of Enkidu's death and the mourning of Gilgamesh for his companion, we are told that Gilgamesh is disturbed by the realization that he himself too must die, 'When I die, shall I not be like Enkidu? Woe has entered my belly. Fearing death, I roam over the steppe.' [12] The only mortal who is known to have escaped death and attained immortality is Gilgamesh's ancestor Utnapishtim, the Babylonian equivalent of Ziusudra, the Sumerian hero of the Flood. Gilgamesh therefore resolves to go in search of his ancestor in order to discover the secret of immortality. He receives various warnings of the difficulties and dangers of the journey. He is told before he can reach his goal he will have to cross the mountains of Mashu and the waters of death, a journey which only the god Shamash has ever accomplished. Nevertheless, he braves the dangers and reaches Utnapishtim at last. The text is broken at the point where the two meet, and when it becomes legible again Utnapishtim is telling Gilgamesh that the gods have reserved to themselves the secret of death and life. Gilgamesh then asks Utnapishtim how he has attained the possession of immortality, and in reply Utnapishtim tells him the story of the Flood. This is contained in the eleventh tablet of the Epic of Gilgamesh, the longest and best preserved of the twelve tablets which comprise the Epic. That the myth was widely known in the ancient East is attested by the fact that Hittite and Hurrian fragments of the myth have been discovered.

Utnapishtim begins by telling Gilgamesh that the story which he is about to relate is 'a hidden matter, a secret of the gods'. He describes himself as a man of Shuruppak, most ancient of the cities of Akkad. Ea reveals to him through the wall of his reed-hut that the gods have decided to destroy all the seed of life by a flood, though the reason for their decision is not given. Ea instructs Utnapishtim to build a ship into which he is to bring 'the seed of all living things'. The dimensions and shape of the ship are given, according to which it appears that the ship was to be a perfect cube. Utnapishtim asks Ea how he is to explain to the citizens of Shuruppak the reasons for his actions, and Ea tells him that he is to say that he has incurred the displeasure of Enlil and that he has been banished from Enlil's territory. He tells them, 'To the Deep I will therefore go down, to dwell with my lord Ea.' He further tells them that Enlil is about to shower down abundance upon them; so that they are completely deceived as to the god's real intentions. Then follows the account of the building of the ship and the loading of it:

> '(Whatever I had) I laded upon her:
> Whatever I had of silver I laded upon her;
> Whatever I (had) of gold I laded upon her;
> Whatever I had of all the living beings I (laded) upon her.
> All my family and kin I made go aboard the ship.
> The beasts of the field, the wild creatures of the field,
>   All the craftsmen I made go aboard.' [13]

Then follows a vivid description of the storm. Adad thunders; Nergal tears down the doorposts of the gates that hold back the waters of the upper ocean; the Anunnaki lift up the torches, 'setting the land ablaze with their glare'. The gods themselves are alarmed and cower like dogs against the wall of heaven. Ishtar, who apparently had incited the gods to destroy mankind, lifts up her voice and bewails her action, while the rest of the gods weep with her. The storm rages for six days and nights. On the seventh day it subsides; Utnapishtim looks out and sees that the landscape is as level as a flat roof, and that 'all of mankind had returned to clay'. The ship grounds on Mt Nisir. Utnapishtim waits seven days, and then sends out a dove which returns having found no resting place. He then sends out a swallow which also returns. Finally he sends out a raven which finds food and does not return. Then he lets out all that are in the ship and offers sacrifice. The gods smell the sweet savour and gather like flies to the sacrifice.

Ishtar arrives, and lifts up her necklace of lapis-lazuli and swears by it never to forget what has happened. She up-braids Enlil for having caused the destruction of her people. Then Enlil arrives at the sacrifices and is furious that any one has been allowed to escape. Ninurta blames Ea for be-traying the secret of the gods, and Ea expostulates with Enlil and intercedes for Utnapishtim. Enlil is appeased and blesses Utnapishtim and his wife and confers upon them immortality like the gods. He decrees that henceforth they shall dwell far away at the mouth of the rivers. There the account of the Flood ends, and the rest of the tablet, to-gether with tablet twelve, belong to the Gilgamesh story, and will be dealt with later.

While excavations at various Mesopotamian sites have shown evidence for severe floods at Ur, Kish, and Erech, there is no evidence for a flood covering the whole country; and the severity and date of the floods differ for each of the above-mentioned cities. Nevertheless the myth undoubtedly rests upon the tradition of a flood of unusual severity, al-though, as its setting in the Gilgamesh Epic suggests, it has been linked up with funerary ritual and with the search for immortality. There is not, however, sufficient evidence to show that the Flood myth, like the Creation myth, became a ritual myth. We shall now describe the other Assyro–Babylonian myths which have been preserved in the various collections which the labours of archaeologists have made available in recent years.

The Epic of Gilgamesh

This very remarkable literary production in which, as we have already seen, the Flood myth is embedded, is partly myth and partly saga. It relates the adventures of a semi-mythical king of Erech who is named in the Sumerian king-lists as the fifth king of the first dynasty of Erech, and is said to have reigned 120 years. The work was extremely popular and widely distributed in the ancient Near East. Fragments of a Hittite translation have been found in the archives of Boghazköy; also a fragment of a Hittite version. A fragment of the Akkadian version was found in the course of the American excavation of Megiddo. Professor Speiser's words about the Epic are worth quoting. 'For the first time in the history of the world a profound experience on such a heroic scale has found expression in a noble style. The scope and sweep of the epic, and its sheer poetic power, give it a timeless appeal. In antiquity, the influence of the poem spread to various tongues and cultures.[14]

The Akkadian version consisted of twelve tablets, of which most of the fragments come from the library of Ashurbanipal at Nineveh. The longest and best preserved fragment is tablet eleven containing the account of the Flood, which we have already discussed. The Epic opens with a description of the strength and heroic qualities of Gilgamesh. The gods have created him of superhuman size and valour; he is said to be two-thirds god and one-third man. But the nobles of Erech complain to the gods that Gilgamesh, who should be the shepherd of his people, is behaving in an arrogant and tyrannical manner. They beg the gods to create a being like Gilgamesh, against whom he may measure his strength, so that they may have peace. Accordingly the goddess Aruru fashions from clay the figure of Enkidu, a wild human creature of the steppes, of surpassing strength. He feeds on grass, is friendly to the wild beasts and drinks with them at their watering-places. He destroys the hunter's snares and delivers the wild animals taken in them. When one of Gilgamesh's hunters brings the report to him of the nature and strange behaviour of this wild man of the steppes, Gilgamesh tells the hunter to take a temple-prostitute to the watering-place where

Enkidu is wont to drink with the wild animals that she may exercise her wiles upon him. The hunter does as he was commanded, and the woman lies in wait for Enkidu until he comes to drink with the wild beasts at the watering-place. When he comes she displays her charms before him, and he is seized with desire for her. After seven days of amorous delight Enkidu awakes from his trance and finds that a change has taken place in him. The wild beasts now flee from him in terror, and the woman says to him, 'Thou art wise, Enkidu, thou art become like a god.' She then tells him of the glories and delights of Erech, and of the strength and fame of Gilgamesh; she induces him to discard his clothing of skins, to shave and anoint himself, and leads him to Erech into the presence of Gilgamesh. Enkidu and Gilgamesh then engage in a trial of strength which ends in a compact of friendship. The two swear eternal comradeship. This ends the first episode of the Epic. Here we are inevitably reminded of the theme of Genesis 3, where the serpent promises Adam that he will become wise and like God, knowing good and evil, if he partakes of the forbidden fruit.

It can hardly be doubted that the Epic in its present form is composed of various myths and folk-stories which have been brought together and artisically welded into a whole round the central figure of Gilgamesh.

The next episode relates the adventures of Gilgamesh and Enkidu as they set out to attack and slay the fire-breathing giant Huwawa, or, as his name is given in the Assyrian version, Humbaba. The purpose of the enterprise is, as Gilgamesh says to Enkidu, 'that all evil from the land we may banish'. It is possible that these stories of the adventures of Gilgamesh and his trusty comrade Enkidu may have helped to shape the Greek myth of the labours of Hercules, though some scholars deny this possibility.[15] In the Epic, Huwawa is represented as guarding the cedar forests of the Amanus stretching six thousand leagues. Enkidu endeavours to dissuade his friend from this perilous enterprise, but Gilgamesh is determined to attempt it, and, with the help of the gods, after a tremendous struggle they slay Huwawa and cut off his head. In the account of this episode the cedar forest is described as being the abode of the goddess Irnini, another name for Ishtar, and this forms the link with the next episode in the Epic.

When Gilgamesh returns in triumph from his victory, the goddess Ishtar is attracted by his beauty and tries to induce him to become her lover. He rejects her advances with insults, and reminds her of the miserable fate of all her previous lovers. Enraged by his rejection, the goddess begs Anu to avenge her by creating the Bull of heaven and sending him to ravage the kingdom of Gilgamesh. The bull is sent down and wreaks havoc among the people of Erech, but is ultimately slain by Enkidu. As the result of this act the gods meet in council and decide that Enkidu must die. Enkidu has a dream in which he sees himself carried off to the underworld and transformed by Nergal into a ghost. The dream contains a description of the Semitic conception of the underworld which is worth quoting:

> 'He (the god) transformed me,
> So that my arms were like those of a bird.
> Looking at me, he leads me to the House of Darkness,
>   The abode of Irkalla,
> To the house which none leave who have entered it,
> On the road from which there is no way back,
> To the house wherein the dwellers are bereft of light,
> Where dust is their fare and clay their food.
> They are clothed like birds, with wings for garments,
> And see no light, residing in darkness.' [16]

Enkidu then falls sick and dies, and we have a vivid description of the grief of Gilgamesh and the mourning ritual which he performs for his friend, reminding one of the mourning rites performed by Achilles for Patroclus. There is a suggestion in the Epic here that death is a new and dreadful experience. Gilgamesh is represented as dreading that he must become like Enkidu, 'When I die, shall I not be like Enkidu? Woe has entered my belly. Fearing death, I roam over the steppe.' He resolves to go in search of immortality, and the account of his adventures during the search constitutes the next section of the Epic. Gilgamesh is aware that his ancestor Utnapishtim is the only mortal who has acquired immortality, and he determines to find him in order to learn from him the secrets of death and life. At the outset of his journey he comes to the foot of the mountain range called Mashu, the entrance to which is guarded by a scorpion-man and his wife. The scorpion-man tells him that no mortal has ever crossed the mountain and braved its dangers, but when Gilgamesh discloses the object of his journey, the guardian lets him pass, and he travels along the sun's road. For twelve leagues he journeys in darkness until he reaches Shamash, the sun-god. Shamash tells him that his quest is vain, 'Gilgamesh, whither rovest thou, The life thou pursuest thou shalt not find.' But he will not be dissuaded and goes on his way. He then comes to the shore of the sea and the waters of death. There he finds another guardian, the goddess Siduri, the ale-wife; she too endeavours to dissuade him from attempting to cross the deadly sea, and tells him that none but Shamash can cross that sea. She tells him to enjoy life while he may in words that strangely resemble the words of the Master of assemblies in Eccl. 9:7–9:

> 'Gilgamesh, whither rovest thou?
> The life thou pursuest thou shalt not find.
> When the gods created mankind,
> Death for mankind they set aside,

Life in their own hands retaining.
Thou, Gilgamesh, let full be thy belly,
Make thou merry by day and by night.
Of each day make thou a feast of rejoicing,
Day and night dance thou and play.
Let thy garments be sparkling and fresh,
Thy head be washed, bathe thou in water.
Pay heed to the little one that holds thy hand,
Let thy spouse delight in thy bosom,
For this is the task of mankind.' [17]

It is hard to resist the conclusion that the late Hebrew moralist was acquainted with this passage in the Epic.

But the hero refuses to listen to Siduri with her jug of ale, and pushes on towards the last stage of his perilous journey. By the shore he meets Urshanabi who had been the steersman of Utnapishtim's boat, and commands him to ferry him across the waters of death. Urshanabi tells him that he must go into the forest and cut down 120 poles each sixty cubits long. He is to use these as punt poles letting each drop as he uses it, so as not to touch the fatal waters of death. He follows Urshanabi's advice, and comes at last to Utnapishtim's dwelling-place. He immediately begs Utnapishtim to tell him how he has attained to the immortality which he himself is so eagerly seeking. In answer his ancestor tells him the story of the Flood, as we have already seen, and confirms what the scorpion-man, Shamash, and Siduri have already told him, that the gods have reserved immortality for themselves and have decreed death as the lot of mankind. Utnapishtim shows Gilgamesh that he cannot even resist sleep, much less the final sleep of death. As Gilgamesh prepares to depart disappointed, Utnapishtim, as a parting gift, tells him of a plant which has the property of making the old young again, but in order to get it he will have to dive to the bottom of the sea.

Gilgamesh does so and brings up the wonder-working plant. On his way back to Erech he stops by a pool to bathe and change his clothes; while he is doing this a serpent smells the odour of the plant and carries it off, sloughing its skin as it goes. This feature of the story is clearly an aetiological myth explaining why the serpent is able to renew its life by casting its old skin. So the quest has failed, and the episode closes with the picture of Gilgamesh sitting by the shore and lamenting his misfortune. He returns empty-handed to Erech, and here the epic probably ended. But, in the form in which we have it now, an additional tablet has been appended, making the twelfth and final tablet. It has been shown by Professors Gadd and Kramer that this tablet is a direct translation from the Sumerian. It has also been shown that the beginning of the tablet is a continuation of another episode in the complex of Gilgamesh myths. This is the myth of Gilgamesh and the Huluppu-tree. It is evidently an aetiological myth explaining the origin of the sacred drum, the *pukku*, and its ritual use. According to this myth, Inanna, who is Ishtar, had taken a huluppu-tree from the banks of the Euphrates, and planted it in her garden, intending to make her bed and chair from its wood. When hostile forces prevented her from carrying out her purpose, Gilgamesh came to her help. In gratitude she gave him a *pukku* and a *mikku* made from the base and crown of the tree respectively. These two objects have been interpreted by scholars as a magic drum and a magic drum-stick. It may be remarked in passing that the big *lilissu*-drum and its drum-sticks played an important part in Akkadian ritual; the description of its making and the rituals which accompanied it is given in Thureau-Dangin's *Rituels accadiens*. Smaller drums were also used in Akkadian ritual, and the *pukku* may have been such a drum.

Tablet twelve opens with Gilgamesh lamenting the loss

of his *pukku* and his *mikku*, which have somehow disappeared into the underworld. Enkidu undertakes to go down into the underworld and recover the lost objects. Gilgamesh advises him as to the observance of certain rules of behaviour in order that he may not be seized and held there. Enkidu breaks all these rules and is seized and held in the underworld. Gilgamesh then appeals to Enlil for help, in vain, then to Sin, also in vain, and finally to Ea who tells Nergal to make a hole in the ground to allow the spirit of Enkidu to ascend. 'The spirit of Enkidu, like a wind-puff, issued forth from the nether world.' Gilgamesh begs Enkidu to describe the order of the underworld and the state of the dwellers therein. Enkidu tells Gilgamesh that the body which he has loved and embraced is devoured by vermin and filled with dust. Gilgamesh throws himself on the ground and weeps. The last part of the tablet is badly mutilated, but it appears to describe the difference between the lot in the underworld of those who have received proper funeral rites and the miserable state of those who have not.

Here the Gilgamesh cycle ends. It clearly embodies a mass of early Sumerian and Akkadian myth and folklore. Some of the myths contained in it come under the head of ritual myths, while several are intended to explain various elements in Mesopotamian beliefs and practices. Underlying the epic as a whole is the theme which underlies several other Akkadian myths, the plaint of the human spirit before the fact of death and the loss of immortality.

The Myth of Adapa

The same theme underlies another myth which seems to have been popular beyond the limits of Mesopotamia, since a fragment of it was found among the Amarna archives in

Egypt. The name of its hero, Adapa, has been equated by the Assyriologist, Ebeling, with the Hebrew name Adam, so that it may be regarded as a myth about the first man. Adapa, according to the myth, was the son of Ea, the god of wisdom. He was priest-king of Eridu, the oldest of the Babylonian cities. Ea had created him 'as the model of man', and had given him wisdom, but not eternal life. His priestly duties are described, and one of these was to provide fish for the table of the gods. One day he was fishing when the South Wind blew and overturned his boat. In rage he broke the wing of the South Wind so that it did not blow for seven days. Anu the high god observed this, and sent his messenger, Ilabrat, to inquire the reason for it. Ilabrat came back and told Anu what Adapa had done. Anu then ordered Adapa to be brought before him. Ea, 'he who knows what pertains to heaven', gave his son advice as to how he should proceed on approaching Anu. He told Adapa to put on mourning apparel and appear with hair disordered. When he reached the gate of heaven he would find it guarded by two gods, Tammuz and Ningizzida. They would ask him what he wanted and why he was in mourning. He was to reply that he was in mourning for two gods who had disappeared from the land, and when they asked him who these gods were, he was to reply, Tammuz and Ningizzida. Flattered by this they would speak favourably to Anu on his behalf and introduce him into the presence of the high god. But Ea warned his son that when he came before Anu, he would be offered bread of death and water of death; these he must refuse. He would also be offered a garment and anointing oil, which he might accept. All these injunctions he was to observe with care.

Everything fell out as Ea had foretold, Adapa gained the favour of the gods who guarded the gate, and was brought before Anu who regarded him with favour and accepted his explanation of what had happened to the South Wind. Then Anu asked the assembled gods what should be done for Adapa, and, presumably with the intention of conferring immortality upon him, ordered bread of life and water of life to be offered to him. Adapa, obeying his father's orders, refused them, but put on the garment which was offered to him, and anointed himself with the oil which they gave him. Thereupon Anu laughed and asked Adapa why he had acted so strangely. When Adapa explained that it was by the advice of his father, Ea, that he had refused what was offered to him, Anu tells him that by his act he has deprived himself of the gift of immortality. The end of the tablet is broken, but it seems that Anu sent Adapa back to earth with certain privileges and disabilities. Eridu was to be freed from feudal obligations, and special dignity was conferred upon its priesthood; but misfortune and disease were to be the lot of mankind, allayed, however, by the ministrations of Ninkarrak, the goddess of healing.

There are various points of interest in this remarkable myth. As frequently in these myths, the loss of immortality is ascribed to the jealousy of one or other of the gods, and the belief is expressed that the gods have reserved immortality for themselves. We also see from this myth that the disappearance of Tammuz is a recurrent element in Semitic mythology. It may be possible to see in the garment which is provided for the hero by the gods a link with the feature in the Hebrew story of the Fall in which Yahweh provides Adam and Eve with garments of skin. There is also the aetiological element explaining the origin of the special exemption from feudal dues enjoyed by the ancient priesthood of Eridu.

The Myth of Etana and the Eagle

Many of the Mesopotamian cylinder seals represent scenes which seem to be concerned with incidents in the myths. Several of them have been thought to represent the exploits of Gilgamesh, but very few of them can be identified with any certainty. There is a special interest in the fact that the myth of Etana can be identified with certainty as depicted on an early seal.[18] In the early Sumerian king-lists the first dynasty after the Flood is the legendary dynasty of Kish, and the thirteenth king of Kish is listed as Etana the shepherd, who ascended to heaven. The seal represents a figure rising from the ground on the back of an eagle, while sheep graze, and two dogs gaze up at the ascending figure.

The motive of several of the myths already dealt with recurs in a different form in the myth of Etana, in this instance connected with birth instead of death. In the course of transmission the myth has become interwoven with a folk-story of the eagle and the serpent. The myth opens with a description of the state of mankind after the Flood, without the guidance and shepherding of a king. The insignia of kinship, the sceptre, crown, tiara, and shepherd's crook are laid up before Anu in heaven. Then the great Anunnaki, the deciders of destiny, decide that kingship shall be sent down from heaven. It is apparently to be inferred that Etana is the appointed king. But in order to secure the permanence of the kingship an heir was necessary, and Etana has no son. We are shown Etana daily offering sacrifices to Shamash and beseeching the god to grant him an heir. He cries to Shamash, 'O Lord, may it issue from thy mouth, grant me the plant of birth, show me the plant of birth, remove my burden, and produce for me a name.' Shamash tells the king to cross the mountain, there he will find a pit and in the pit an eagle imprisoned. He is to free the eagle, and the eagle will guide him to the plant of birth.

Here the myth introduces the folk-story of the eagle and the serpent. According to the story, at the beginning of things the eagle and the serpent had sworn a solemn oath of friendship. The eagle had his nest and his young in the top of a tree, while the serpent and his young lived at its base. They undertook to protect and provide food for each other's young. For a time all went well. But the eagle conceived evil in his heart, and broke his oath; while the serpent was away hunting, the eagle devoured the serpent's young. When the serpent returned and found his home desolate, he appealed to Shamash for vengeance against the oath-breaker. Shamash showed him how to snare the eagle, break his wings, and imprison him in a pit. Here the eagle lay, miserably crying in vain to Shamash for help. Here, directed by Shamash, Etana enters, and delivers the eagle, who, in gratitude for his help, promises to carry him up to the throne of Ishtar from whom he may obtain the plant of birth. This is the point of the story depicted by the cylinder seal. The myth vividly describes the stages of the ascent, as the landscape diminishes and disappears. In the middle of the description of the descent the tablet breaks off; but as the king-list gives the name of Etana's son and successor, the myth presumably had a fortunate ending.

It may be remarked that the folk-tale of the eagle and the serpent contains one of the oldest elements of that type of literature. It represents the youngest of the eagle's children as possessing wisdom, and warning his father against the danger of breaking his oath. The myth also suggests an underlying birth ritual, just as traces of funerary rituals appear in the Gilgamesh Epic.

Mesopotamian Myths

The Myth of Zu

This is another of the few myths which have an identifiable pictorial representation on cylinder seals.[19] The myth also represents another aspect of the theme of life and death which we have already seen so frequently recurring in the Akkadian myths. Zu is shown on the seals as a bird-like figure. Frankfort calls him a bird-man, but he is rather to be regarded as one of the lesser deities, possibly an underworld god, who, like the monstrous offspring of Tiamat, is an enemy of the high gods. His name frequently occurs in ritual texts, and always as in conflict with the great gods. Another theme of this myth, also found in the myth of Etana, is the importance and sacral character of Akkadian kingship.

The myth, in the mutilated form in which we have it, begins with the announcement that Zu has stolen the tablets of destiny which are the insignia of kinship. We have already seen in the Epic of Creation that Marduk wrested from Kingu the tablets of destiny and thereby established his supremacy among the gods. Zu is said to have stolen them from Enlil while he was washing, and to have flown away to his mountain. There is dismay in heaven, and the gods deliberate in council as to who shall be entrusted with the task of vanquishing Zu and recovering the tablets. The whole scene closely resembles the similar scene in the Epic of Creation. Various gods are invoked, but decline the task, and finally it appears that Lugalbanda, the father of Gilgamesh, undertook the mission and slew Zu and regained possession of the tablets. In a hymn of Ashurbanipal we find Marduk named as the god 'who crushed the skull of Zu'.

In one of the texts known as ritual commentaries, a footrace is mentioned as forming part of the ritual of the Baby-

Ionian New Year Festival, and the race is explained as signifying the conquest of Zu by Ninurta. In the ritual of making the sacred *lilissu*-drum, translated by Thureau-Dangin in his *Rituels accadiens*, the slaying of a black bull takes place, and before the bull is slain the priest utters a spell into each ear of the bull. In the incantation whispered into the right ear of the bull, the victim is addressed as 'Great Bull that treadest the celestial herbage', while in the other ear he is addressed as 'Spawn of Zu'. Hence it is clear that this curious myth played an important part in the ritual traditions of Babylon.

Before we leave the subject of the Akkadian myths one more short but interesting myth may be added. It may serve as an illustration of the way in which myth material might be taken up and used in apotropaic incantations and exorcisms. The Tammuz myth was widely used in this way, and in the example here given the myth of Creation is used.

The Worm and the Toothache

The Babylonians believed that the various diseases to which the inhabitants of the delta were subject were due to the attacks of evil spirits, or to the malice of wizards or witches. Hence while such remedies as were known were used in the treatment of bodily ailments, the treatment was always accompanied by the recitation of one or more incantations. The colophon at the end of this incantation says that it should be repeated three times over the sufferer after the prescribed treatment has been applied. The translation here given is Speiser's in *The Ancient Near Eastern Texts*, p. 100:

Mesopotamian Myths

After Anu had created heaven,
Heaven had created the earth,
The earth had created the rivers,
The rivers had created the canals,
The canals had created the marsh,
And the marsh had created the worm,
The worm went weeping before Shamash,
His tears flowing before Ea:
'What wilt thou give me for my food?
What wilt thou give me for my sucking?'
'I shall give thee the ripe fig,
And the apricot.'
'Of what use are they to me, the ripe fig
And the apricot?
Lift me up and among the teeth
And the gums cause me to dwell!
The blood of the tooth will I suck,
And of the gum I will gnaw
Its roots!'
    Fix the pin and seize its foot.*
'Because thou hast said this, O worm!
May Ea smite thee with the might
Of his hand!'

* This is the instruction given to the dentist.

1. Pritchard, J. B. (Ed.), *The Ancient Near Eastern Texts relating to the Old Testament*, pp. 52 ff.
2. Witzel, M., *Tammuz Liturgien und Verwandtes.*
3. Kramer, S. N., *Sumerian Mythology*, p. 61.
4. Pritchard, J. B., op. cit., p. 44.
5. Frankfort, H., *The Intellectual Adventure of Ancient Man*, p. 138.
6. Kramer, S. N., op. cit., pp. 102 ff.
7. Smith, S., *Early History of Assyria*, p. 334.
8. Pritchard, J. B., op. cit., p. 108.

9. *Ibid.*, p. 107.
10. Ezek. 8 : 14.
11. Frankfort, H., op. cit., p. 171.
12. Pritchard, J. B., op. cit., p. 88.
13. *Ibid.*, p. 94.
14. *Ibid.*, p. 72.
15. Smith, S., op. cit., p. 35.
16. Pritchard, J. B., op. cit., p. 87.
17. *Ibid.*, p. 90.
18. Franfort, H., *Cylinder Seals*, pp. 138–9 and Plate XXIVh.
19. *Ibid.*, pp. 132 ff. and Plate XXIIIf.

Chapter 2

EGYPTIAN MYTHOLOGY

WHILE there are certain underlying resemblances between
the mythology of Egypt and that of Sumer and Akkad, the
differences are more striking and important. There is a
superficial resemblance between the physical conditions
under which the two civilizations developed their mythology. Both countries lay in river valleys, and the way of
life of each was largely dominated by the character of its
river. The proximity of extensive deserts has also left its
stamp upon the mythology of both countries.

But the configuration and the behaviour of the great river
of Egypt are totally unlike those of the Tigris–Euphrates
river system. The course of the Nile divides Egypt into two
regions, the Valley and the Delta. From the first cataract
down to Memphis, the present Cairo, the Nile runs for 500
miles between the steep walls of the great rift in the Libyan
plateau, watering a narrow strip of alluvial soil, ranging
from six to twelve miles in width. North of Memphis the
scene changes abruptly. The cliffs diverge, and the Valley
spreads like a great fan, sixty miles long with an arc of
400 miles in length, through which the Nile discharges
itself into the Mediterranean by innumerable arms. The
French scholar, Moret, has said, 'So nature has created a
Mediterranean Egypt and an African Egypt. The difference
between these "Two Lands", as the Egyptians called them,
are great enough to make a marked impression on the
mythological and human history of the country.'[1] When we
come to describe the mythology of Egypt we shall find how
profoundly this division between Upper and Lower Egypt

and the forces which brought about the union of the 'Two Lands' into one united monarchy have left their mark on almost every aspect of Egyptian belief and practice. The vital necessity of a central control over the distribution of the flood waters of the Nile brought a united kingdom into existence in Egypt long before the city states of Sumer and Akkad had been forced into some kind of unity under the first Amorite dynasty.

Hence kingship assumed a very different form in Egypt from that which it acquired in the city states of Sumer and Akkad. The Sumerians believed that 'kingship was sent down from heaven', as we have seen in the myth of Etana. The Sumerian, and later the Babylonian and Assyrian, kings declared themselves to be chosen and appointed by the gods. They acted as representatives of the gods in the rituals, and in some cases were deified after death. But in Egypt the king did not represent the god, he was the god. While he lived he was Horus, and when dead he was Osiris, lord of the dead. Hence a great deal of Egyptian myth is concerned with kingship and the Osiris–Horus cycle. Closely connected with the Osiris cult and its mythology was the Egyptian preoccupation with death and the after-life leading to the unique development of mummification and its attendant myth and ritual.

Side by side with the cult of Osiris, and possibly more ancient in origin, was the cult of Re the sun-god, round whom another cycle of myths collected. In the course of time, the two cults became closely interwoven, bringing about a fusion of the Osirian myths with those of the sun-god.

The third central element in Egyptian religion was the Nile whose influence on every aspect of Egyptian life was all-pervading. The river of Egypt was worshipped as a god and had a place in Egyptian ritual and mythology to which the rivers of Sumer and Akkad can offer no parallel. The extreme fluidity of the Egyptian religion, and the confusing way in which the myths and attributes of the various gods merge into one another, make it hard to give a clear pattern of Egyptian mythology. Hence, in order that our account may present some kind of order we shall group the myths of Egypt under the three heads mentioned above, those connected with Osiris, with Re, and with the Nile.

THE OSIRIAN MYTHS

Three main themes underlie the complicated system of rituals and myths which have the figure of Osiris as their centre. First, there is a political element. The myth of the conflict between Osiris and his brother Seth reflects the course of the struggle which ultimately made Upper and Lower Egypt a united monarchy. Secondly, there is the agricultural element. Osiris is a vegetation god. Like Tammuz he is a dying and rising god who dies with the dying vegetation and returns to life with its rebirth. Thirdly, there is the eschatological element. Osiris is Khent-Amenti, Lord of the underworld. He presides over the tribunal which decides the fate of the departed souls, and in this aspect he is inseparably connected with the complicated ritual of mummification.

The outline of the myth of Osiris is contained in Plutarch's treatise *De Iside*, and it is generally agreed that Plutarch's account is drawn from early Egyptian sources such as the Pyramid Texts. According to this account Osiris was a culture hero who taught the ancient Egyptians the arts of agriculture and metal-working. In the myth, Osiris was the son of Geb, the earth-god, and his sister and wife was the goddess Isis, who ruled over Egypt with him and assisted him in his beneficent activities. In the twenty-eighth year of his reign Osiris was slain by his brother Typhon, Plutarch's name for the god Seth. At a feast Seth, with seventy-two fellow conspirators, induced Osiris, for a jest, to allow himself to be shut up in a chest which was then thrown into the Nile. The chest floated down the river through the Tanitic mouth into the Mediterranean, and was carried to Byblos. It is with reference to this element in the myth that Osiris is called 'the drowned one' in the Pyramid Texts. Isis, seeking her husband in grief, found the chest at Byblos, and brought back the body in a coffin to Buto. According to the myth as Plutarch relates it, when the chest containing the body of Osiris landed at Byblos, a sycamore tree grew up round the chest and enclosed it. The king of Byblos, admiring the size and beauty of the tree, ordered it to be cut down and made into a pillar for his palace. Isis found and recognized what the pillar contained, and begged it from the king of Byblos. The myth goes on to tell how Seth, hunting by moonlight, found the coffin containing the body of Osiris, and cut the corpse into pieces and scattered them throughout the land of Egypt. Once more Isis renewed her search and recovered all the scattered members of her husband, except the *membrum virile* which had been devoured by the oxyrhynchus fish. She put the limbs together, and, with the assistance of her sister, the goddess Nephthys, performed magic ceremonies over the body and restored it to life. The risen Osiris, however, did not remain on earth, but became the king of the 'western region', the place of the departed spirits. The next phase of the myth concerns the avenging of Osiris by his son Horus. According to the myth Isis conceived Horus of the dead Osiris by magical means. The young Horus, who is often represented in Egyptian art as a child seated on a lotus bud, devoted himself to the avenging of his father, and the vindication of his own legitimacy. Various passages in the Pyramid Texts describe the prolonged struggle between Horus and his followers and Seth and his followers. In the fight between Horus and Seth, Horus lost one of his eyes, an astral element in the myth, representing the period of the moon's disappearance. The following passage describes the triumph of Horus over Seth:

O Osiris, Horus is come, and embraces thee. He caused Thoth to turn back from thee those of the followers of Seth, and he brought them to thee in bonds. He made the heart of Seth to fail, for thou art greater than he, thou wast born before him, thy virtue surpasses his. Geb saw thy merits and set thee in thy place. Horus caused the gods to join thee, and to be brotherly with thee. He caused the gods to avenge thee. Then Geb set his sandal upon the head of thy enemy, who retreats far from thee. Thy son Horus struck him, he saved his eye from his hand, and gave it to thee; thy soul is within, thy power is within. Horus has caused thee to grip thy enemies, so that they cannot escape from thee. Horus has gripped Seth, and placed him beneath thee, that he may bear thee and tremble under thee. O Osiris, Horus has avenged thee.[2]

Other passages from the same source describe the vindication of Osiris before the tribunal of the gods, presided over by Geb, and the proclamation of the legitimacy of Horus, to whom the kingdom of Upper and Lower Egypt is assigned by the decree of the gods. This is, in outline, the Osiris-Horus myth. It is nowhere brought together in a single literary form, like the Akkadian Creation Epic, but has to be pieced together from various sources. In addition to the astral element mentioned above, the myth reflects the prolonged struggle between Upper and Lower Egypt for predominance, ending in the unification of the two regions into one kingdom. The original duality was preserved in many ways in the constitution of Egypt, and was symbolized by the fact that the Pharaoh wore the united crowns, the white and the red, of Upper and Lower Egypt on ceremonial occasions. An aetiological element is to be noted in the explanation of the institution of the royal brother-sister marriage which remained customary in Egypt down to Ptolemaic times and the end of the monarchy. It must also be noted that many features of the myth were represented in ritual. The resurrection of Osiris was enacted in ritual by the ceremony of the raising of the *djed*-tree, representing the sycamore tree of the myth. Also, in the month Athyr, the women made clay images of Osiris and cast them into the Nile, representing the drowning of Osiris in the myth.

THE MYTHS OF RE, THE SUN-GOD

In Egypt the cult of the sun-god occupied a far more important place than it did in the ritual and mythology of Sumer and Akkad. Shamash was the guardian of justice, but he was never one of the great triad of gods, nor was he associated with myths of creation. But in Egypt Re, according to tradition, was the first king of Egypt, and as Atum he was the creator of the world. As its name indicates, the city of Heliopolis was the chief centre of the cult of Re, and it was probably there that the fusion of the cult of Osiris with that of the sun-god took place during the Old Kingdom period. From that point in the history of Egypt the cartouches, which were the traditional form in which the ceremonial titles of the Pharaohs were inscribed, contained a throne name indicating that the king was the son of Re. The Horus-falcon that is to be seen protecting the head of the Pharaoh Khafre on his statue,[3] shows the identification of Horus with Re, and the association of the kingship with Re. We also find that the Osiris-Horus mythology, fused with the cult of Re, determines the order of the accession and coronation of the Pharaoh. The death of Tuthmosis III and the accession of Amenhotep II are thus described:

> King Tuthmosis III went up to heaven,
> He was united with the sun disc;
> The body of the god joined him who had made him.
> When the next morning dawned
> The sun disc shone forth,
> The sky became bright,
> King Amenhotep II was installed on the throne of his father.[4]

We have already seen that the dead king became Osiris, and the text just quoted shows that he also became united with Re. It is clear that the mythology of Re and of Osiris have become completely blended. There are, however, some elements of the solar mythology which remain distinct from the Osiris myth.

Creation Myths

Owing to that fluidity of Egyptian religion of which we have already spoken, the creation myth assumes many forms. Underneath them all lies the basic experience of the sun's action upon the slime left by the receding waters of the Nile flood. While there is an Egyptian myth of the slaying of a dragon, to which we shall refer later, this is not connected with creation, as it is in the Akkadian Epic of Creation. The earliest form of the myth, modified later by the theologies of Heliopolis and Memphis, presents the sun-god, Atum-Re, seated upon the primeval hillock, and bringing into existence 'the gods who are in his following'. But Atum himself is depicted as rising out of Nun, the primeval ocean. In the form of the myth which belonged to

Hermopolis, in Middle Egypt, the emergence of Atum was due to the activity of the Ogdoad. These were conceived of as animal forms, four snakes and four frogs, representing primeval chaos. Their names were Nun and his consort Naunet, Kuk and Kauket, Huh and Hauhet, and, lastly, Amon and Amaunet. Atum, emerging from the waters, brings these elements of chaos into order, so that they appear in the texts as gods functioning in their proper places. An early form of the myth, according to the Pyramid Texts, represents Atum as fertilizing himself and producing Shu and Tefnut, air and moisture; from the union of this pair came Geb and Nut, the earth-god and the sky-goddess; here the Heliopolitan theology introduced the figures of the Osirian group, and made Geb and Nut give birth to Osiris and Isis, side by side with Seth and Nephthys, thus completing the Heliopolitan Ennead.

Another form of the myth arose from the desire of Memphis to vindicate its importance as the new capital of the first dynasties of Egypt. Ptah was the local god of Memphis, and the Memphite Theology, as the document which contains this form of the myth is usually called, transformed the Heliopolitan Ennead by giving the primacy in the activity of creation to Ptah. In that part of this remarkable text which concerns creation, Ptah is equated with Nun, the primeval ocean, and is presented as bringing Atum and all the gods of the Heliopolitan Ennead into existence by his divine word. What might be called the creed of the Memphite Theology is briefly summarized in the following passage of the text:

> Ptah who is upon the Great Throne,
> Ptah-Nun, the father who begot Atum;
> Ptah-Naunet, the mother who bore Atum;
> Ptah the Great, that is, the heart and tongue of the Ennead
> (Ptah) who gave birth to the gods.[5]

Egyptian Mythology

In the Egyptian concrete way of thinking, the heart and the tongue represent thought and speech, the attributes of the creator, and are deified as Horus and Thoth. By his thought and speech Ptah brings the gods into existence, brings order out of chaos; like Marduk he fixes the destinies, provides food for mankind, divides Egypt into provinces and cities, and assigns their places to the various local gods. This description of Ptah's creative activities closes with the words, 'And so Ptah rested (or, was satisfied), after he had made everything', a phrase which cannot fail to suggest a comparison with the closing words of the Priestly account of creation in Genesis 1. The identification of Ptah with Atum-Re constitutes the link between the Heliopolitan myth of Re as creator and the Memphite Theology which takes the myth as the basis for cosmological speculation of great subtlety. It is interesting to note that the creation of man occupies no special place in Egyptian mythology. We have representations of Khnum fashioning mankind on the potter's wheel,[6] and there are various references in Egyptian texts to this special creative activity of the god Khnum, but the line between man and the gods is not so sharply drawn as it is in Semitic religion, hence the comparatively slight emphasis in Egyptian mythology on the creation of man.

The Old Age of Re

While the flooding of the Nile could at times be excessive, there was nothing in Egyptian experience which corresponded to the destructive floods of the Tigris and Euphrates. Hence there is no Egyptian myth of the destruction of mankind by a flood. But we have a myth of a destruction of mankind connected with Re. According to this myth Re grew old and felt that his authority over gods and men was failing. He summoned an assembly of the gods and told them that men were plotting against him. He asked the advice of Nun, the eldest of the gods, and Nun advised that the Eye of Re, in the form of the goddess Hathor, should be sent against mankind. Hathor began the slaughter, and waded in blood. But, apparently, Re did not desire the complete destruction of mankind; so he devised a plan for the making of seven thousand jars of barley beer, dyed with red ochre to resemble blood. This was poured out on the fields to a depth of nine inches. When the Goddess saw this flood shining in the dawn, reflecting her own face in its beauty, she was allured and drank and became drunk, and forgot her rage against mankind. So mankind was saved from complete destruction. The text in which this myth is preserved seems to have been used as a magical incantation to protect the body of a dead king. It may also have an aetiological element as an explanation of the origin of barley beer.

The Slaying of Apophis

Many magical texts contain references to the overthrow or slaying of the serpent Apophis, the enemy of Re. In one text Seth is the agent of the victory, much as Marduk is the agent of the gods in the conquest of the dragon Tiamat in the Akkadian myth. In another the gods to whom Re has given birth employ their magical powers to destroy Apophis. A passage from one of the magical papyri describes this activity of the gods, 'When (these gods) rich in magic spoke, it was the (very) spirit (*ka*) of magic, for they were ordered to annihilate my enemies by the effective charms of their speech, and I sent out those who came into being from my body to overthrow that evil enemy (i.e., Apophis)'.[7] Then follows a detailed description of the completeness of the destruction. Another text containing a curse against the enemies of the Pharaoh says, 'They [i.e., the king's enemies] shall be like the snake Apophis on New Year's morning.' [8] Here the snake symbolizes the darkness which the sun defeats every morning as he begins his journey in his heavenly barque through the heavens, and especially on New Year's morning. We have here an interesting parallel with the victory of Marduk over the dragon Tiamat at the Babylonian New Year Festival.

The Secret Name of Re

Another interesting solar myth concerns the magical potency of the name of a god. According to this myth, Isis set her heart upon learning the secret name of Re in order that she might use it in her magic spells. To this end she created a snake and placed it in the path by which Re would come forth from his palace. When Re came out the snake bit him, and Re was seized by burning pains. He summoned the assembly of the gods who came in mourning, and among them was Isis with her magic skills. Re told them what had happened to him, and begged Isis to relieve him. Isis said that in order to make her spell efficacious she must know his name. Re told her that he was Khepri in the morning, Re at midday, and Atum in the evening, but Isis said that none of these was his secret name of power, and his pains remained unrelieved. Finally he revealed his secret name on condition that it was made known to no god but Horus. Then Isis, using Re's name of power, uttered the spell which removed the effects of the snake's poison. The text ends with directions for the use of the spell to cure snake-bite.

The Egyptian myths connected with Re are too numerous to describe in full detail, but one more curious myth may be cited here.

Thoth as the Deputy of Re

According to this myth, Re orders Thoth to be summoned before him. When he appears Re tells him that he is to be Re's deputy and give light in the underworld, while Re shines in his proper place in the heavens. Re says, 'Behold ye, I am here in the sky in my proper place. Inasmuch as I shall act so that the light may shine in the Underworld and the Island of Baba, thou shalt be scribe there and keep in order those who are in them, those who may perform deeds of rebellion against me, the followers of this dissatisfied being [possibly a reference to Apophis]. Thou shalt be in my place, a Place-taker. Thus thou shalt be called Thoth, the place-taker of Re.' [9]

This is an aetiological myth intended to explain why the moon gives light at night. The darkness is the abode of the enemies of Re and of the underworld demons. In the myth Thoth is constituted a moon god as the deputy of Re. In the pre-dynastic period Thoth was the god of the ibis nome, and the same myth goes on to explain, by the kind of pun to which the Egyptians were much addicted, how the ibis came to be the symbol of Thoth.

NILOTIC MYTHS

The Nile naturally occupies a large place in the mythology of Egypt. We have already seen that the tendency of Egyptian thought was both conservative and comprehensive. The Egyptians never discarded anything, but blended earlier and rival systems into a synthesis, as we have seen taking place with the Osirian and Re mythology. Hence we find the myths which are connected with the Nile closely bound up with the mortuary rituals and myths of the Osiris cult, as well as with the cult of Re.

The river was worshipped as a god under the name of Hapi. There is a famous statue of the Nile-god in the Vatican Museum which represents the god reclining, holding ears of corn and a cornucopia, and surrounded by sixteen children, each a cubit high. This symbolizes the fact that if the Nile flood fell below sixteen cubits there would be famine. On a tomb at Abydos we have a representation of the two Niles bringing papyrus, lotus, and various kinds of food and drink. The myth of the two Niles is contained in Akh-en-Aton's famous hymn to the Aton, or Sun-disc. In this it is proclaimed that Aton creates a Nile in the underworld and brings it forth to sustain the people of Egypt. He also creates a heavenly Nile to give water for the foreign peoples. But the most important and significant aspect of Nilotic mythology is that associated with the Osiris myth. In a hymn to Osiris Rameses IV says, 'Thou art the Nile, gods and men live from thy outflow.' We have seen that one of the elements in the Osiris myth was the drowning of Osiris and his finding by Isis. Plutarch relates that in the month of Athyr the priests went down to the river by night and filled a golden vessel with sweet water. As they did so the attendant people cried, 'Osiris is found.' [10] Both the drowning and the finding of Osiris in the Nile play an important part in the seasonal rituals of Egypt. The turning points in the annual rising and falling of the Nile were mythologized as the drowning or death of Osiris, his finding by Isis, and his resurrection through the magical arts of Isis and Nephthys, and each detail of the myth was enacted in rituals whose scene was the Nile. Nor must it be forgotten that all this Osiris–Nile mythology and ritual was inseparably connected with the functions of kingship in Egypt.

Middle Eastern Mythology

Here our survey of Egyptian mythology must cease. What has been presented here is only a selection from the vast and intricate mass of Egyptian mythology.

1. Moret, A., *The Nile and Egyptian Civilization*, p. 26.
2. Erman (trans.), *Pyramid Texts*, pp. 575 ff.
3. Frankfort, H., *Kingship and the Gods*, frontispiece.
4. *Ibid.*, pp. 102–3.
5. Pritchard, J. B., *The Ancient Near Eastern Texts relating to the Old Testament*, p. 5.
6. Pritchard, J. B., *The Ancient Near East in Pictures relating to the Old Testament*, p. 569.
7. Pritchard, J. B., *The Ancient Near Eastern Texts relating to the Old Testament*, p. 7.
8. Frankfort, H., op. cit., p. 24.
9. Pritchard, J. B., op. cit., p. 8.
10. Plutarch, *De Iside*, p. 59.

Chapter 3

UGARITIC MYTHOLOGY

FROM the mythologies of the two great civilizations of
Babylon and Egypt, we turn now to the intermediate region
of Canaan, inhabited entirely by Semitic-speaking peoples.
Until the first quarter of the present century very little was
known about the mythology of Canaan except fragments
of tradition preserved in the writings of late Greek historio-
graphers, such as Philo of Byblos. But the discovery of the
now well-known Ras Shamra Tablets in 1928, on the site
of the ancient north Syrian city of Ugarit, mentioned in
Egyptian, Babylonian, and Hittite records, threw a flood of
light on this hitherto unexplored territory. Among the large
quantity of tablets discovered at Ras Shamra, or Ugarit, was
a group written in a script which appeared to be cuneiform,
but which was unfamiliar to the cuneiform experts. The
small number of the signs employed suggested that the
script might be alphabetic, and it was very soon found that
this surmise was correct. The tablets in question proved to
be written in an alphabet of twenty-eight letters, and in a
language hitherto unknown. This language, now known as
Ugaritic, has been shown to belong to the Semitic group,
and is closely related to Arabic, Aramaic, and Hebrew.
References in the tablets made it possible to assign them to
a date in the fourteenth century B.C., but there is no doubt
that the Canaanite myths and legends which they contain
are much earlier in origin. Many of the tablets are broken,
and the text is often uncertain, presents many obscurities,
and needs to be used with caution. Nevertheless, the main

outlines of the myths are sufficiently established for it to be possible to give a reliable account of them.

The Canaanite myths and legends contained in these tablets fall into three groups. The largest group is concerned with the adventures and exploits of the god Baal and his relations with the other members of the Canaanite pantheon. It may be remarked that the names of many of these gods and goddesses are familiar to us from the Old Testament, and fragments of Ugaritic mythology have been traced in Hebrew poetry.

The second cycle consists of the Epic of Keret, king of Hubur. The poem may have an historical basis, as we have seen to be the case with the Epic of Gilgamesh. But the mythological element in it is hard to distinguish from the legendary, and we can hardly omit it from an account of Canaanite mythology.

The third cycle consists of the tale or legend of Aqhat, the son of Danel, another legendary Canaanite king. This story, like the preceding one, has so much mythical material in it that it must be included here.

THE MYTHS OF BAAL

The seven tablets which contain the myth, or myths, of Baal are in such an imperfect condition that it is impossible to determine the original order of the tablets or to discover whether the various episodes which they relate ever formed a connected narrative such as we have in the Babylonian Epic of Creation. Moreover, as the texts are written without vowel points, and the language, although clearly Semitic, is still imperfectly understood, much remains obscure, and scholars differ considerably, both in their translations and in their interpretations of the Ugaritic material. Comparison between the earlier translations of Virolleaud, and the more recent versions of Ginsberg, Gaster, Gordon, and Driver, shows on the one hand how widely translations may differ, and on the other hand that a considerable amount of agreement has been reached. The episodes selected here to illustrate the character of the Baal myth are those about which general agreement has been reached among scholars.

The Myth of Baal and the Waters

In this episode the personages who appear are the high god El, often styled the Bull El, the Father of the gods, who dwells in the field of El, at the sources of the rivers; his son, Baal, the god of fertility, often called 'the rider of the clouds', and as god of lightning and thunder sometimes called Hadad; then there is the god of the seas and rivers, Yam-Nahar; between him and Baal there is a feud, Yam-Nahar being favoured by El, while Baal is in revolt against his father El. Other figures are the craftsman-god, Kothar-u-Khasis who appears in several of the Baal myths; the sun-goddess Shapash (the Ugaritic form of the Akkadian Shamash), often called the Torch of the gods; Ashtoreth, the wife of El and mother of the gods; Asherah, the Lady of the Sea, who covets the throne of Baal for her son Ashtar; and Anath, the sister of Baal, who plays an important part in many of the Baal myths.

In the myth which we are now describing, Yam-Nahar sends envoys to the council of the gods to demand that Baal be delivered up to him. The gods bow their heads in fear, and El promises that Baal shall be handed over to the messengers of Yam-Nahar. Thereupon Baal taunts the gods for their cowardice and attacks the messengers, but is restrained by Anath and Astoreth. Then Kothar-u-Khasis arms Baal with two magic weapons, called 'Yagrush' (Chaser) and 'Aymur' (Driver). Baal attacks Yam-Nahar with Yagrush and strikes him on the chest, but Yam is not subdued; then he strikes Yam on the forehead with Aymur and fells him to the earth. He then proposes to make an end of Yam, but is restrained by Ashtoreth who reminds him that Yam is now their captive. Baal is ashamed and spares his vanquished enemy. In the symbolism of the myth Yam-Nahar in his arrogance represents the hostile aspect of the sea and the rivers, threatening to overflow and devastate the earth, while Baal represents the beneficent aspect of the waters as rain. Baal rides the clouds, sending lightning and thunder to show his power, but also dispensing the kindly rains in their season to make the earth fertile. When we come to deal with Hebrew mythology we shall see how much of the Baal myth was taken over by the Hebrews and transferred to Yahweh when they settled in Canaan. In another form of the myth Baal's conquest of the forces of disorder and chaos is depicted as the slaying of the seven-headed dragon Lotan (the Hebrew Leviathan), where there seems to be evidence of the influence on Canaanite mythology of the Akkadian myth of the slaying of the dragon Tiamat by Marduk.

Anath's Slaughter of Baal's Enemies

This episode appears to be connected with the myth of Baal's conquest of Yam-Nahar, and has echoes of the Egyptian myth of the destruction of mankind by Hathor (see p. 74). Baal's sister, the goddess Anath, orders a great feast to be prepared in celebration of Baal's victory over Yam-Nahar. The feast is held in Baal's palace on Mt Zaphon, the mountain of the gods in 'the sides of the north'. This site is frequently mentioned in Hebrew poetry as a divine abode

(cf. Ps. 48 : 2). Having adorned herself with rouge and henna
for the feast, Anath closes the doors of the palace and proceeds to slay all the enemies of Baal. She girds herself with
the heads and hands of the slain, and wades in blood up to
her knees. This last detail occurs in the story of Hathor's
slaughter of Re's enemies.

The Building of a House for Baal

It will be remembered that after Marduk's victory over
Tiamat, the Epic of Creation gives an account of the building by the gods of the temple Esagila for Marduk. Similarly,
after Baal's victory over Yam-Nahar, the god complains that
he has no house like the other gods. He and his sister Anath
beg the Lady Asherah of the Sea that she will intercede with
El and obtain permission for the building of Baal's house.
Asherah accordingly saddles her ass and journeys north-
wards to Mt Zaphon, to the pavilion of El. She flatters El
and obtains his permission for Baal to have a house built.
There is some obscurity here in the text, but it appears that,
although Baal already has a house of cedar and brick, he
does not consider it worthy of the position among the gods
to which he aspires. His sister Anath hastens to inform him
of El's permission, and declares that he must have a house
of gold and silver and lapis-lazuli.

Messengers are then sent to the craftsman-god Kothar,
who comes and is received with great honour and is feasted.
A curious debate then ensues between Baal and Kothar on
the question whether the new house is to have a window
or not. Kothar insists that the house should have a window,
but Baal refuses to allow it, on the ground, apparently, that
he does not wish Yam to be able to spy out Baal's con-
cubines. However, Kothar ultimately prevails, and the
house is furnished with a window through which Baal is

able to send lightning and thunder and rain. The completion of the building is celebrated by a great feast to which Baal invites all his kinsfolk and the seventy children of Asherah. At the feast Baal declares his supremacy and announces that he will not send tribute to El's new favourite, the god Mot, the god of sterility and the underworld. This introduces a new figure in the Baal mythology, and the next episodes are concerned with the struggle between Baal and Mot. Having overcome the challenge of the waters, personified by Yam, Baal must now defeat the threat to the fertile earth by the encroachment of the barren steppe, personified by Mot. There is a probable connexion between the name Mot and the Hebrew word *môt* which means 'death'. It has been suggested that in Ps. 48:14 there is an allusion to Mot; instead of the Authorized Version rendering of the last clause of the verse, 'He will be our guide, even unto death', some scholars would render, 'He will lead us against Mot'.[1]

Baal and Mot

The tablets containing the account of Baal's conflict with Mot are very imperfect and obscure. Further study and the discovery of fresh material may elucidate some of the present obscurity. What is here given rests upon the general agreement of the Ugaritic experts.

Baal has apparently sent messengers, Gapn and Ugar, to Mot refusing tribute. They return with a threatening message from Mot which fills Baal with dread, and he sends back a humble reply, 'Be gracious, O divine Mot; I am thy slave, thy bondman for ever.' Mot rejoices and declares that Baal is humbled for ever. Then we are told that messengers arrive at the field of El and announce that they have found Baal lying dead, but what caused his death is not told. From

what follows it can be inferred that Baal is in the underworld, like Tammuz. At the news El descends from his
throne and sits on the ground, pours dust on his head, puts
on sackcloth, and gashes his cheeks with a stone. He utters
lamentations over Baal. Anath goes wandering in search of
her brother, and having found his body, with the help of
Shapash she carried it up to Zaphon, buries it, and makes a
great funeral feast in his honour. It is to be inferred that
Baal's absence from the earth lasts for seven years, years of
drought and famine. Anath then seizes Mot, splits him with
her sword, winnows him with her fan, burns him with fire,
grinds him in her hand-mill, and sows him in the ground –
actions which clearly symbolize the various things which
are done to the corn.

After a break in the text we learn that El dreams that
Baal is alive. He laughs for joy, and lifts up his voice and
proclaims that Baal lives; he shouts the news to the virgin
Anath and to Shapash. But, though it is assumed that
Baal lives, no one knows where he is, and the cry goes
out, 'Where is puissant Baal?' 'Where is the Prince, the
Lord of earth?' During Baal's absence in the underworld
the question of his successor had been raised, and Asherah
puts forward her son Ashtar as a claimant for the vacant
throne. Ashtar accordingly ascends the throne, but finds
that his feet do not reach the footstool, nor does his head
reach its top. So he descends from the throne and declares
that he cannot rule in the heights of Zaphon.

We then have a description of the parched condition of
the soil because of Baal's absence, and Shapash, the Torch
of the gods, goes in search of the missing god. The concluding scene of what may be called the Baal-Mot epic represents Baal re-assuming his throne in Zaphon and renewing
the conflict with Mot who appears to have come to life
again. There is a terrific struggle; the two gods gore each

other like bulls, kick each other like stallions, and both fall to the ground. Shapash separates the combatants and some sort of reconciliation takes place; Baal resumes his throne and rewards his supporters. The poem ends with a colophon giving the name of the scribe, and the name of the king of Ugarit, Niqmad, in whose reign the poem was written down. This enables us to date the writing down of the poem in the Amarna epoch, in the middle of the fourteenth century B.C. But the material of the poem is probably much more ancient. Ugarit lay within the sphere of influence of both Assyrian and Egyptian civilizations, and these north Canaanite myths show clear signs of both Akkadian and Egyptian mythology.

There are two other myths connected with Baal which do not form part of the Baal Epic, but which cannot be omitted in an account of Ugaritic mythology.

The Myth of Hadad

The tablet containing this myth is badly broken and very obscure. Moreover, it is not certain whether the tablet contained the whole of the myth. However, enough of the meaning has been extracted to give us some additional details of the cycle of Baal myths. Hadad is another name for Baal in his character of the god of thunder and lightning. The name is frequently found in the Old Testament, for example, in the theophorous names of the Syrian kings, Ben-hadad and Hadad-ezer. In this myth the handmaidens of the goddess Asherah, the Lady of the Sea, and of Yarikh, the moon-god, are sent to entreat the help of El against the attacks of monstrous creatures sent by Baal which are devouring them like worms. El tells them to go into the wilderness and hide themselves, and there give birth to wild beasts with horns and humps like buffaloes. Baal-Hadad will see

them and chase after them. They do so and Baal is seized
with desire to hunt the creatures to which they have given
birth. But the chase proves disastrous to the god; he is
caught by the monsters and disappears for seven years, sunk
in a bog and helpless. During his absence things fall into
chaos on earth. His brethren go in search of him and find
him with joy. The myth is evidently another version of the
death of Baal and Anath's search for him. It also reflects the
Sumero-Akkadian myth of the descent of Tammuz into the
underworld and Ishtar's descent thither to deliver him.

Anath and the Buffalo

This fragment is of interest because it establishes the fact
that bestiality, a practice which was punishable by death
among the Hebrews, was sanctioned among the Canaanites
as having sacral significance. The myth represents Anath
as inquiring where Baal is to be found, and being told by
his servants that he is away hunting. She follows after him,
and when she finds him he is overcome with love for her.
He then has intercourse with her in the form of a cow. The
fragment ends with the announcement to Baal by Anath
that, 'A wild ox is born to Baal, a buffalo to the Rider of
the Clouds.' Puissant Baal rejoices. The myth also reflects
the practice of brother-sister marriage which was the rule
in Egypt for the marriage of the Pharaohs. The Greek myth
of Zeus and Io may have its roots in this Canaanite myth.

THE LEGEND OF KERET

This curious story is preserved in three tablets, two of which
are in a good state of preservation while the third is imperfect. There are gaps, and it is possible that some further

tablets are missing. However, there is general agreement about the main outlines of the story, though scholars differ considerably about its interpretation. Some think that it has an historical basis,[2] while others see in it a cult legend with a strongly mythical character.[3] It has been suggested [4] that the poem was composed to glorify King Niqmad of Ugarit by giving him a deified ancestor, the Keret, King of Hubur, who is the subject of this poem. The mythological element is sufficiently prominent to justify its inclusion in an account of Canaanite mythology.

According to the legend or myth, Keret, King of Hubur, has suffered the loss of his wife, his children, and his palace. As he bewails his wretched condition, El appears to him in a dream and orders him to put off his mourning, wash and anoint himself, and ascend a high tower where he is to offer a sacrifice to El. He is then to prepare for an expedition against a city called Udom, which some scholars have identified with the Biblical and historical Edom. The king of Udom, Pabil, will offer to buy him off with vast wealth, but he is to refuse such offers and demand Pabil's daughter, Huriya, in marriage. Keret carries out El's instructions, and on the way to Udom he makes a vow to Asherah of Sidon to give her much gold and silver if she will prosper his enterprise. Keret succeeds in forcing Pabil to give him his daughter, and the marriage is celebrated with a great feast. All the gods of Ugarit attend the banquet, and El blesses Keret over a cup of wine, and promises him seven sons and a daughter. One of his sons will be suckled by the goddesses Asherah and Anath, to qualify him to succeed Keret on the throne. These promises are fulfilled, but Keret fails to fulfil his vow to Asherah, and disasters follow, which are to be understood as due to the wrath of Asherah. Keret falls ill and seems to be at the point of death. One of his sons, Elhu, is much distressed; he had believed his father to be of divine descent and immortal. It is also suggested that, as the result of the king's illness, rain is withheld and crops are threatened, a theme which we have met with in the Baal epic. Keret tells Elhu not to waste time condoling with him, but to send for his sister, Thitmanat, whose name means 'the eighth one',[5] and who is full of pity. She is to join with Elhu in preparing a sacrifice to El; Elhu makes an offering of oil to Baal in order to procure a return of fertility to the land. Lutpan, i.e., El, calls seven times upon the assembled gods to discover if any of them can find a cure for Keret's sickness. When none of them can do so, El announces that he himself will cast a spell to drive out the plague, and pinches off a piece of dung for this purpose. Here there is a break in the tablet; it next appears that El has sent out a goddess of healing, whose name is Shataqat, to fly over a hundred cities and towns to find a release for Keret from his sickness. She is successful, and word goes out that she has been victorious over death. Keret's appetite returns and he resumes his seat on his throne. Meanwhile the eldest son, Yassib, has been planning to usurp his father's place, and goes in to Keret's sick-room and tells him that he is about to descend into the pit. Yassib demands that Keret shall come down from his throne and yield up his authority to himself. Here the poem ends with a tremendous curse invoked upon Yassib by his outraged father.

Some substratum of historical tradition may underlie this curious legend, but it is clear that it is mainly mythological, and some parts of it suggest connexion with ritual.

THE LEGEND OF AQHAT

As much of this legend as has been preserved is contained on three tablets, two of which are in good condition, the third being badly damaged. There is, however, general agreement among the Ugaritic experts about the main outlines of the story. Virolleaud's *editio princeps* bore the title 'The Legend of Danel', but later study of the text showed that Danel's son Aqhat was the hero of the poem, and its theme is the death and resurrection of Aqhat.

In the opening scene of the poem King Danel, or Daniel, is shown feasting the gods in order to obtain a son. Baal intercedes with El on behalf of Danel, and El promises that he shall have a son. The news is brought to Danel who rejoices and goes in to his wife; she conceives and bears a son who will continue Danel's line and perform all the necessary filial duties.

Danel is then shown dispensing justice to widows and orphans in the threshing-floor; the craftsman-god Kothar-u-Khasis is seen approaching, bringing with him a bow and arrows. The king orders his wife to prepare a feast for Kothar and his companions, and in the course of the feast he persuades his divine visitor to give him the bow and arrows which he then lays on the knees of his son.

It next appears that the goddess Anath, having seen Aqhat's skill with the bow, wishes to possess it, and offers Aqhat much gold and silver for it. Aqhat refuses to part with it, and advises her to get one like it made for herself. The goddess persists and promises to give Aqhat immortality like Baal if he will yield up the bow to her. Aqhat rejects her offer with contumely, saying that she cannot confer immortality upon man whose destiny is to die, and adding that the bow is a man's weapon not to be wielded by a woman. Anath then flies to El and, with threats which sound oddly as addressed to the king of the gods, obtains permission to carry out her plans for gaining possession of Aqhat's bow. She then goes to Yatpan, who seems to be some kind of minor deity of a war-like nature, and proposes to change him into a vulture (or eagle), so that he may fly over Aqhat while he is eating and strike him down and get possession of the bow. It appears, however, that the goddess does not intend Aqhat to be killed, but only rendered unconscious. Yatpan, in carrying out Anath's plan, kills Aqhat, but although he carries off the bow it is broken and lost, or perhaps falls into the water, and Anath is frustrated of her desire. She weeps over the death of Aqhat and says that she will restore him to life, so that he may give her the bow and arrows, and that fertility may be restored to the earth, for it appears that the death of Aqhat, like the death of Baal, has caused drought and failure of the crops.

Here a new figure appears on the stage, Pughat, or Paghat, the sister of Aqhat. She has seen the vultures over the threshing-floor and the signs of sterility in the land, and entreats Danel to do something about it. All his measures fail, and there is drought and famine for seven years, just as there was in the Baal epic. Messengers arrive bringing the news that Aqhat is dead, slain by Anath; Danel vows vengeance on the murderer of his son. He prays to Baal to enable him to find out which of the vultures has devoured Aqhat's remains, that he may recover them and give them decent burial. Baal brings down the vultures one by one, until Danel finds his son's remains in Sumul, the mother of the vultures. He curses the three cities which lie in the neighbourhood of Aqhat's murder, and then returns to his palace and mourns for Aqhat for seven years. Meanwhile Pughat endeavours to carry out her plan of vengeance, and proposes to employ Yatpan as her agent, being unaware of his part in the slaying of Aqhat. The legend should end with the resurrection of Aqhat, but it is clear that some tablets are missing.

One of the titles frequently applied to Danel is 'man of Rapha'. There are three fragmentary tablets, one of which contains a reference to Danel, the man of Rapha, and which are concerned with the activities of some beings called Repum. The tablets also contain a reference to the coronation of Baal; thus linking up Danel the man of Rapha, the Repum, and Baal; but they do not seem to belong to the legend of Aqhat. They are mentioned here because they have some connexion with Hebrew mythology. There are several references in the Old Testament to the Rephaim,[6] (a) as the dead or shades, and (b) as a race or tribe inhabiting Canaan before Hebrew settlement there. In the fragments referred to, the Repum are invited, apparently by El, to a feast and a sacrifice, which seem to be connected with the return of Baal from the underworld and his coronation. The Repum seem to be eight in number, under the leadership of a figure who has the title of Repu-Baal. They come to the feast in chariots, or riding on horses and asses. Hence it seems difficult to regard them as ghosts or shades, although they are so represented in Driver's and Gordon's translations of these obscure texts. The most attractive interpretation is that put forward by Dr John Gray [7] who sees in them cultic functionaries associated with the king, who were concerned with the rituals intended to secure the fertility of the fields, and who had a special part to play at the festival of the enthronement of Baal. Hence these three fragments may contain a ritual myth which was recited at some such festival as the tablets describe.

There are two more Ugaritic myths which call for mention.

THE BIRTHS OF DAWN AND DUSK
(SHAHAR AND SHALIM)

This curious text shows every sign of being a ritual myth. It is divided by lines into episodes which are accompanied by rubrics giving directions for the performance of ritual acts. The poem or hymn begins with an invocation to the gracious gods which is several times repeated. The gracious gods are the twin gods, Shahar and Shalim, whose birth the myth describes. In order to avert evil influences from the birth an apotropaic ritual is performed in which an image of Mot, the god of sterility, is subjected to beating and opprobrious treatment. Then preparatory rituals are described, among which is the cooking of a kid in milk, a ritual which was forbidden in the early Hebrew sacrificial regulations.[8] Then various rituals take place which are intended to increase the potency of El, who proceeds to impregnate the goddesses, Asherah and Rahmaya. They first give birth to the twin gods, Shahar and Shalim, and then to a second pair of gods who appear to be sea-gods. Gaster has suggested [9] that we have here the text of a ritual performed at a Canaanite feast of first-fruits in early summer.

THE MYTH OF NIKKAL AND THE KATHIRAT

This poem describes the marriage of Nikkal, the goddess of the fruits of the earth, daughter of Hiribi, the god of summer, to Yarikh, the moon-god. The wise goddesses, the Kathirat, are summoned to provide the things necessary for the wedding, and the announcement is made of the rich gifts which Yarikh will provide as the bride-price. Driver has suggested that the Kathirat may correspond to the Graces of Greek mythology.[10] They are mentioned in connexion with the marriage of Danel, and are described as 'swallows', because swallows are connected with fertility and childbirth.[11] Hiribi appears to act as an intermediary, and suggests other possible brides for Yarikh, but the divine bridegroom declares himself determined to have no other bride but Nikkal. The weighing-out of the bride-price is described, and the poem ends with an invocation to the Kathirat who celebrate the marriage with joyful songs. It has been suggested that the poem is an epithalamium for a mortal bride, and that what has been taken to be the name of the youngest of the Kathirat is the name of the real bride.[12] This is possible; but if so, the occasion would probably be a royal wedding, and the poem celebrating it may be compared with a similar royal epithalamium in Hebrew poetry, Ps. 45.

In bringing this account of Ugaritic mythology to an end it must be remarked that the texts from which it is drawn are in a very imperfect condition and without vowel points, so that much remains obscure, and translations are often conjectural. Nevertheless the account here given represents the general agreement of scholars on the main outlines and significance of these interesting myths. They show clear evidence of the influence of both Egyptian and Babylonian mythology, the latter predominating. It has also been established that Canaanite mythology has left marked traces in Hebrew poetry and mythology.

1. Johnson, A. R., *Sacral Kingship in Ancient Israel*, p. 81.
2. Langhe, R. de., *Myth, Ritual, and Kingship*, pp. 122 ff.
3. Engnell, I., *Studies in Divine Kingship*.
4. Gordon, C. R., *Ugaritic Literature*, pp. 66–7.
5. Driver, G. R., *Canaanite Myths and Legends*, p. 4.
6. Isa. 14:9; 24:14. 19; Ps. 88:10; Pro. 2:18; 9:18; 21:16; Gen. 14:5; Deut. 2:11 *et. al.*
7. Gray, J., 'The Rephaim' (*Palestine Exploration Quarterly*, 1949).
8. Exod. 23:19.
9. Gaster, T. H., *Thespis*, pp. 97–8.
10. Driver, G. R., op. cit., p. 24.
11. Harrison, J. E., *Themis*, pp. 97–8.
12. Driver, G. R., op. cit., pp. 24–5.

Chapter 4

HITTITE MYTHOLOGY

UNTIL the middle of the last century all that was known of the Hittites was that they were mentioned in the Old Testament in the lists of peoples inhabiting Canaan before the Israelite settlement. Abraham bought the cave of Machpelah from Hittites in the neighbourhood of Hebron, and the approach of their army caused the Syrians to raise the siege of Samaria during the Omri dynasty.[1] The prophet Ezekiel reproached the inhabitants of Jerusalem with being of Hittite descent.[2] But within the last half-century, Winckler's excavation of Boghaz-köi, the site of Hattusas, the ancient capital of the Hittite empire, and the labours of many scholars in deciphering and translating the Hittite cuneiform script, has shown that the Hittites (a name which they did not use of themselves), were non-Semitic invaders who settled in Asia Minor about the beginning of the third millennium B.C., and built up an empire which lasted until 1225 B.C. and played a very important role in the politics of the ancient Near East. More than 10,000 tablets were found in the archives of Boghaz-köi, and this important body of literature included interesting mythological material, of which some account must now be given. Hittite studies are still in their infancy, comparatively speaking, and more myths than have so far been discovered may yet come to light; but those already made available to us by skill of Hittite scholars show the influence of the Babylonian religion, although they have a very distinctive character of their own. They contain much more of the folklore element than those we have so far described, and the ancestry of some familiar European folk tales and *Märchen* can be traced back to these curious myths and legends.

Those who may wish to know more of the origins, religion, literature, and art, of the Hittites will find an admirable and authoritative account in Dr O. R. Gurney's Pelican Book entitled *The Hittites*.

The three myths given here to illustrate the character of Hittite mythology have been translated by Professor Albrecht Goetze, and may be found in full in Pritchard's indispensable collection entitled *Ancient Near Eastern Texts Relating to the Old Testament*, to which frequent reference has already been made.

THE MYTH OF ULLIKUMMIS

Underlying this myth is the familiar motive which we have already encountered in Akkadian and Ugaritic myths, the rivalry between older and younger gods. Anus, who is the Akkadian Anu, the sky god, has ousted his father Alalus from the throne, and has in turn been pulled down by his son Kumarbis. Certain things happen in the course of Kumarbis's struggle with Anus which result in the birth of the storm-god, and the perennial contest between father and son is renewed. The myth begins by representing Kumarbis as plotting means to create a rival to the storm-god. He sends his messenger, Imbaluris, to the Sea to seek her advice. She summons Kumarbis to her house and makes a feast for him. As the result of her advice, Kumarbis sends his vizier, Mukisanus, to the Waters. What follows is not clear; we next hear that Kumarbis has begotten a son, possibly from the earth goddess. He calls him Ullikummis and sends Imbaluris to the Irsirra deities, perhaps gods of the underworld, with orders that they are to take Ullikummis

to the dark earth and place him upon the right shoulder of
Ubelluris, where he is to grow into a gigantic pillar of
diorite. Ubelluris is a god who, like Atlas, sustains the world
on his shoulders. The growth of Ullikummis is then described; he rises from the sea like a tower until his height is
9,000 leagues and his girth 9,000 leagues. He reaches up to
heaven, to the consternation of the gods. Hebat, the wife of
the storm-god, is driven from her temple. She sends a message to her husband, and he goes to seek help from Ea in
his house, Apsu. Here the borrowing from the Akkadian
Epic of Creation is evident. In the assembly of the gods, Ea
asks why they are allowing mankind to be destroyed by this
monstrous creature. Enlil does not know what is happening. Ea journeys to Ubelluris, who is also unaware of the
extra burden which he is carrying, and turns him round so
that he can see the diorite man standing upon his right
shoulder. Ea then appeals to the older gods to bring the
ancient copper knife which had divided heaven from earth
out of the storehouses of the gods. These are the words of
Ea : 'Listen ye, Olden gods, ye who know the olden words!
Open ye the ancient storehouses of the fathers and fore-
fathers! Let them bring the olden seals of the fathers and
let them seal them up again with them afterwards. Let them
bring forth the olden copper knife with which they severed
heaven from earth. Let them cut through the feet of Ullikummis, the diorite man, whom Kumarbis has fashioned as
a rival to oppose the gods.'[3] Ea then announces to the
assembly of frightened gods that he has crippled Ullikummis, and urges them to go forth and do battle with the
giant. The storm-god mounts his chariot and rides out to
encounter Ullikummis. Here the tablet is broken, but it
would no doubt have described the victory of the storm-
god. There seems to be an echo here of the vision in the
book of Daniel describing the destruction of Nebuchad-

nezzar's great image by the stone cut out of the mountain without hands. There the stone smites the image on its feet of iron and clay and destroys it.[4] The myth also presents another version of the myth of the destruction of mankind and its frustration by the interposition of Ea.

THE MYTH OF ILLUYANKAS

This myth exists in an older and a later version, and is concerned with the slaying of the dragon, Illuyankas. Like the previous myth it contains many folklore motifs. The introductory note to the older version says that it is the cult legend of the Purulli Festival of the storm-god of heaven, and that this version is no longer told. The festival referred to is probably the New Year Festival, and the myth has affinities with the myth of the slaying of the dragon Tiamat, celebrated in the Babylonian Epic of Creation.[5] In the older version, the storm-god is defeated by the dragon, Illuyankas. He appeals to the assembly of the gods for help, and the goddess Inaras prepares a trap for the dragon. She fills many vessels with wine and various kinds of drink, and invites a man named Hupasiyas to help her. He agrees to do so on condition that she will sleep with him. Accordingly she allows him to sleep with her; then she hides him near the dragon's lair, beautifies herself, and entices the dragon to come out with his children. They drink all the vessels dry, and are unable to return to their den. Then Hupasiyas comes out of his hiding-place, binds the dragon with a rope, and the storm-god comes with the rest of the gods and kills the dragon Illuyankas. Then comes an episode which seems to have no connexion with the rest of the myth and is pure folklore. Inaras builds herself a house on a cliff in the land of Tarukka, and instals Hupasiyas in it. She warns him not to look out of the window while she is away, because, if he does so, he will see his wife and children. After she has been away for twenty days he looks out of the window and sees his wife and children. When Inaras returns, Hupasiyas begs to be allowed to go back to his wife and children, whereupon the goddess kills him for his disobedience. The rest of this version is obscure, but there seems to be an allusion to the central place of the king in the Purulli Festival. The theme of the love of an immortal for a mortal and the mortal's desire to return to his own country is one which occurs in the folklore of many countries.

The later version of the myth has some features which are not found in the earlier version. When the dragon defeated the storm-god he took away his heart and his eyes, a detail which has an echo in the Egyptian myth of the fight between Horus and Seth in which Horus lost one of his eyes. In order to be revenged on the dragon, the storm-god took the daughter of a poor man to wife and begot a son by her. When this son grew up he married the daughter of the dragon Illuyankas. The storm-god told his son that when he went to the house of his wife he was to ask for his father's heart and eyes. He did so and they gave him the heart and eyes which he then restored to his father. When the storm-god had recovered his lost members he armed himself and went out to battle with the dragon; as he was on the point of vanquishing him, his own son cried out, 'Count me with him, spare me not.' So the storm-god slew the dragon, Illuyankas and his son as well, and thus was revenged upon the dragon. There is a long break here, and when the text is resumed it appears to deal with a ritual in which there is some competition or race, as the result of which the rank and order of the gods is established. In the ritual commentary on the Babylonian New Year Festival there is a mention of a foot-race in which Marduk's son,

Nebo, vanquishes the god Zu, an incident connected with the resurrection of the dead god. Hence both versions suggest that the Babylonian myth of the slaying of the dragon Tiamat which was recited at the New Year Festival has influenced the Hittite ritual myth of Purulli.

THE MYTH OF TELEPINUS

This myth deals with the same theme as the myth of Tammuz in the underworld, and the disappearance of Baal in the Ugaritic myth. The disappearance of the god produces a failure of every kind of fertility, both of vegetation and of cattle. The myth appears to have been current in several forms, and more than one god, including the sun-god, disappears, but the main text, upon which the account here given is based, has the god Telepinus as its hero. This myth also may be classed among the ritual myths, since it includes the ritual for securing the return of the vanished god.

The beginning of the text is broken so we do not know the causes of the god's anger. The thread of the story is taken up at the point where the rage of Telepinus is described. He is depicted as putting his left shoe on his right foot and his right shoe on his left foot, implying that he was so angry that he did not know what he was doing. Telepinus goes away into the steppe and is lost. He is overcome with fatigue and falls asleep. Then we have a description of the effects of his absence: a mist covers the country; in the fire-place the logs are stifled; at the altars the gods are stifled; the sheep neglects its lamb, and the cow neglects its calf; there is drought and famine so that men and gods perish from hunger. The storm-god becomes anxious about his son Telepinus, and the search begins. The sun-god sends

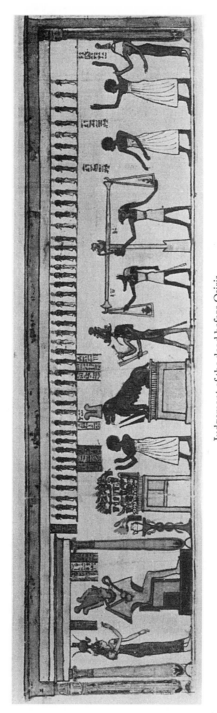

Judgement of the dead before Osiris

The Sky-goddess Nut

Osiris standing in his shrine

Ptah enthroned, king kneeling before him

The God Horus as a hawk

The Goddess Isis

The God Khnum

a. The Goddess Hathor

b. Ta-weret, the hippopotamus
Nile-goddess

Fight between two demons

Guardian deities performing a magical ceremony

The Slaying of the Seven-headed Hydra

a. The Ascent of Etana

b. The Judgement of Zu before Ea

a. The Liberation of the Sun-god

b. The Slaying of Tiamat

13

a. The Goddess Ninhursag and the rain. The slaying of the bull

b. Sun-god slays bull-man. Fire-god burns Kingu

c. Hero and bull-man (Gilgamesh and Enkidu?)

14

The Hittite weather-god Teshub

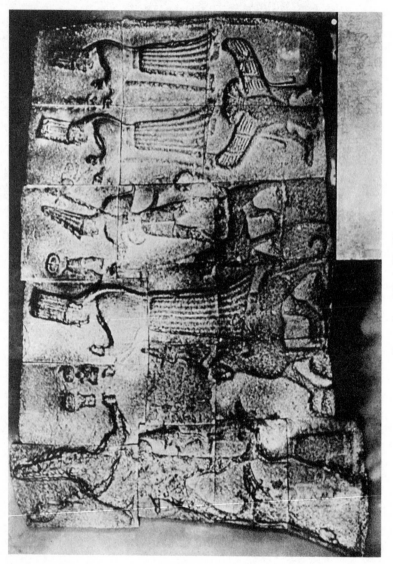

Procession of Gods (Yasilikaya)

out the swift eagle with orders to search every mountain and valley, but the eagle returns unsuccessful. Then the goddess Hannahannas urges the storm-god to do something about it. He goes to the house of Telepinus and batters at the gate. He only succeeds in breaking his hammer, but does not find the missing god, and retires from the quest. Then Hannahannas suggests sending out the Bee in search, but the storm-god mocks at the idea and says that the Bee is too small to succeed in an enterprise in which the great gods have failed. Hannahannas, however, sends out the Bee with orders to sting Telepinus on his hands and feet, to smear wax on his eyes and feet, and purify him and bring him back to the gods. The Bee finds him after a long search and carries out the orders of the goddess. Telepinus is aroused from his sleep, but is more enraged than ever, and the gods are at a loss. Then the sun-god says, 'Fetch man! let him take the spring Hattara on Mount Ammuna. Let him make him move! With the eagle's wing let him make him move!' [6] Some kind of ritual seems to be implied here, but the meaning is obscure. After a break in the text, in which the goddess Kamrusepas, the goddess of healing, seems to have been summoned, her ritual of purification is described. Telepinus returns, borne on the eagle's wing and accompanied by thunder and lightning. Kamruspas calms him and soothes his rage. She orders a sacrifice of twelve rams. Torches are kindled and extinguished, symbolizing the extinction of the god's fury. A spell is then pronounced, apparently by the man mentioned previously, intended to banish all the evils of the rage of Telepinus into the underworld. The concluding words of the spell run, 'The door-keeper has opened the seven doors, has unlocked the seven bolts. Down in the dark earth there stand bronze cauldrons, their lids are of *abaru* metal, their handles of iron. Whatever goes in there comes not out again; it perishes therein.

Let them also receive Telepinus's rage, anger, malice, and fury! Let them not come back!' [7] The text ends with the return of Telepinus to his house and the restoration of prosperity. Telepinus cares for the king and the queen and provides them with enduring life and vigour. An interesting feature of the conclusion of the ritual is the erection of a pole before the god, from which the fleece of a sheep is suspended. The closing lines of the text explain that the pole with its suspended fleece signifies fat of the sheep, grains of corn, wine, cattle, sheep, long life, and many children.

A parallel to the pole erected before Telepinus may be seen in the pole decorated with foliage often depicted in Assyrian and Babylonian seals with attendant figures on each side of it engaged in some kind of ritual act. The raising of the *ded* tree in the Osiris ritual may also be mentioned in this connexion.

These are the principal Hittite myths. Other fragmentary myths have been found of which Dr Gurney has given an account in his excellent Pelican book *The Hittites*, but those here related will give sufficient illustration of the character of Hittite mythology. They show clear dependence upon Babylonian mythology, and also show how much of Greek and Western mythology and folklore has its roots in this curious Hittite material.

1. 2 Kings 6:6.
2. Ezek. 16:3, 45.
3. Pritchard, J. B., *The Ancient Near Eastern Texts, Relating to the Old Testament*, pp. 124–5.
4. Dan. 2:34.
5. See p. 44.
6. Pritchard, J. B., op. cit., p. 127.
7. *Ibid.*, p. 128.

Chapter 5

HEBREW MYTHOLOGY

IN dealing with the literature of Israel we are on much firmer footing than we have been in the case of much of the ancient material with which we have hitherto been concerned. The Sumerian language still presents many difficult problems for the translator, and the unpointed text of the Ugaritic tablets, as well as their mutilated condition, present formidable barriers to the full understanding of the myths and legends which they contain. But the literature of Israel, covering a period of nearly a thousand years, has come down to us in a state of remarkable preservation; so that the meaning of the text itself is, in the main, free from serious difficulties of translation. That the Old Testament contains an abundance of mythological material is undeniable, and it presents problems which do not arise in connexion with the mythologies of the nations by whom Israel was surrounded.

Underlying the sagas of the book of Genesis it is possible to trace the tradition of the two earliest movements of peoples into Canaan which form the beginning of the history of Israel. The first of these under the leadership of Abraham, who is called 'the Hebrew' in the early sources, came from Ur of the Chaldeans about the middle of the eighteenth century B.C. and finally settled in the neighbourhood of Hebron. The second movement, somewhat later, consisted of nomad, or semi-nomad, Aramaeans, under the leadership of Jacob, also called Israel, the eponymous ancestor of the Israelites; this branch ultimately settled around Shechem. A third wave of Hebrew settlement, consisting partly of tribes who had fled from Egypt after a long period of settlement there, entered Canaan from the south and east towards the end of the thirteenth century B.C. All these groups which ultimately became the people of Israel were composed of pastoral people, and in entering Canaan they found themselves in a country already inhabited by a long-established population, Semites like themselves, but whose economy was almost entirely agricultural. The account already given of the mythology of the Canaanites shows the type of religion and ritual practised by agriculturists, and it was to such a type of religious practice that the new-comers had to adapt themselves. The late and somewhat tendentious account of Hebrew settlement given in the book of Joshua suggests that extermination was the declared policy of the invading Hebrews; but earlier accounts, and the testimony of the prophets of Israel, suggest that Canaanite agricultural rituals and seasonal feasts were taken over by the new-comers and persisted, in spite of prophetic protests, until the Exile. In the form in which we have it now, the Old Testament is the product of editorial activity extending over many centuries. In the course of this activity many things were suppressed or modified as the conceptions of the nature of Yahweh developed through the teaching of the prophets. The mythological material was specially affected by this process; hence three main problems confront us in studying the mythology of the Old Testament. First we have to inquire what was the source and original form of the myths which we find there; then what modifications did the Hebrew writers or editors make in the mythical material which they borrowed from Canaanite or other sources; and lastly whether Israel produced any myths of its own.

The final editors of the Old Testament collected most of the mythological material into the first eleven chapters of

Genesis; but other myths and legends are to be found in fragmentary form scattered through the sagas and poetry of Israel and will be dealt with in due course.

CREATION MYTHS

In the first two chapters of Genesis there are two stories of Creation, representing two different stages of the development of the religion of Israel. The first is contained in Chapter 1–2:4^a, and the second in Chapter 2:4^b–25. The first has been assigned by the general agreement of scholars to the editorial activity of writers after the Exile, while the second has been assigned to a much earlier period in the history of Israel, possibly about the beginning of the monarchy. It shows signs of editorial activity, but in its present form it seems to bear the impress of a single mind. The differences between the two accounts may be best seen by setting them out in tabular form:

CHAPTER 1–2:4^a	CHAPTER 2:4^b–25
The original state of the universe is a watery chaos.	The original state of the universe is a waterless waste, without vegetation.
The work of creation is assigned to Elohim, and is divided into six separate operations, each belonging to one day.	The work of creation is assigned to Yahweh Elohim, and no note of time is given.
The order of creation is:	*The order of creation is:*
(*a*) Light.	(*a*) Man, made out of the dust.
(*b*) The firmament – heaven.	(*b*) The Garden, to the east, in Eden.

(c) The dry land – earth. Separation of earth from sea.

(c) Trees of every kind, including the Tree of Life, and the Tree of the Knowledge of Good and Evil.

(d) Vegetation – three orders.

(d) Animals, beasts, and birds (no mention of fish).

(e) The heavenly bodies – sun, moon, and stars.

(e) Woman, created out of man.

(f) Birds and fishes.

(g) Animals and man, male and female together.

In addition to these two main accounts of Creation, there are various references in Hebrew poetry to the divine activity in Creation which suggest that other forms of the myth of Creation may have been current in Israel.

(a) In Ps. 74:12–17 we have an account of how Yahweh, in a contest with the waters, smote the many-headed Leviathan, and then proceeded to create day and night, the heavenly bodies, and the order of the seasons. We have already seen [1] that in the Akkadian Epic of Creation Marduk's slaying of the chaos-dragon Tiamat is followed by his ordering of the universe, and by the building of Esagila. It is also accepted by the majority of scholars that in the Hebrew word *tᵉhôm* used to denote the abyss of waters in Gen. 1:2 there is a reference to the chaos-dragon Tiamat, a point to which we shall return later. But in the passage from Ps. 74 the name of the water-dragon, Leviathan, is the same as the Ugaritic Lotan, the dragon slain by Baal.[2] Hence it is possible that the Hebrew poet was acquainted with the Canaanite form of the myth. We have also seen that another variant of the struggle of Baal against the forces of destruction was the conflict with Mot, which finally ended in the victory of Baal.[3] A reference to this feature of the Ugaritic myth has been seen in Ps. 48:14 which reads in the Revised Version, 'For this God is our God for ever and ever : he will be our guide even unto death'. But the verse has been rendered, 'Our God who abideth for ever is our leader against Death (Hebrew *mot*)', and connected with the Ugaritic myth.[4] This makes it probable that the passage from Ps. 74 is connected with the same source, although, unless we regard the myth of the building of a house for Baal as symbolic of creative activity, no Ugaritic myth of Creation has hitherto been discovered.

(b) In Ps. 104 which is a meditation on Yahweh's activity in Creation, a number of features of the Creation myth occur. Leviathan is mentioned, although not, apparently, as an enemy. Yahweh lays the beams of his chambers in the waters, where we have a parallel to the watery abode of Ea. He rides upon the clouds, an epithet of Baal in the Ugaritic texts. There is a reference to the creation of the sun and the moon and the ordering of the seasons.

(c) Traces of the Creation myth which are not dependent on the two main versions found in Gen. 1 and 2 occur in Job 38, one of the finest pieces of Hebrew poetry, probably of late post-exilic date. Here we find Yahweh described as laying the foundations of the earth on sockets, 'when the morning stars sang together, and all the sons of God shouted for joy', a feature of the myth which has no parallel else-where in the Old Testament, but which finds an echo in the rejoicing of the gods over the victory of Marduk in the Akkadian Epic of Creation, and also in the feast prepared by Baal for the gods and goddesses to celebrate the building of his palace. We also have the taming of the sea, to which Yahweh says, 'Hitherto shalt thou come, but no further; and here shall thy proud waves be stayed' (verse 11). There are two references to Leviathan in Job : a cryptic allusion to those 'who are skilful to rouse up Leviathan' (3:8), and a description of Leviathan in Chapter 41 which is generally understood to be a reference to the crocodile. Here the monster has become completely demythologized. The former reference seems to suggest the use of Leviathan in magical spells. Under the name Rahab, 'the arrogant one', in 26:12–3, we find another reference to the slaying of the chaos-dragon, the taming of the sea, and the ordering of creation, 'He stilleth the sea with his power, and by his understanding he smiteth through Rahab. By his spirit the heavens are beauty (or, adorned); his hand hath pierced the swift (or, fleeing) serpent'. It is clear that in the book of Job the pattern of the ancient myth of Creation has disintegrated and become poeticized.

(d) Finally, the myth of the chaos-dragon passes into eschatology in the writings of the post-exilic prophets. In Isa. 27:1, an oracle, introduced by the characteristic formula 'in that day', declares, 'Yahweh with his sore and great and strong sword shall punish Leviathan the swift serpent, and Leviathan the crooked (or, winding) serpent, and he shall slay the dragon that is in the sea.' Again, in Isa. 51:9–10, we find another transmutation of the same myth. It has become historicized as a symbolic reference to the deliverance of Israel from Egypt: 'Awake, awake, put on strength, O arm of the Lord, as in the days of old, the generations of ancient times. Art not thou it that cut Rahab in pieces, that pierced the dragon? Art not thou it that dried up the sea, the waters of the great deep; that made the depths of the sea a way for the ransomed to pass over?'

We may now return to the two versions of the Creation which the editor of Genesis has placed side by side in the beginning of that book. It should be remarked that, although the Graf-Wellhausen Documentary hypothesis which analysed the Pentateuch into a number of literary sources denoted by the symbols J–E, D, H, and P, has been abandoned by one school of Old Testament scholars, and considerably modified by others, it still remains a useful means of distinguishing the different strata in the Pentateuch and the early historical books. In the case of the two narratives of Creation which we are now considering, the first is usually indicated by the symbol P and assigned to the priestly editors who collected and arranged the traditions of Israel after the Exile. The second is denoted by the symbols J–E, and is regarded as the joint work of the Yahwist and the Elohist, names which indicate two schools (or, possibly individual writers), who were active in the early period of the monarchy, editing the ancient traditions of Israel, preserved either in oral or written form. The symbols refer to the use of the names Yahweh and Elohim used by the two schools respectively. We shall now consider these two versions separately and compare their characteristics. As the second is the earlier of the two, it will be considered first.

The J–E Version. We can see from the comparative table on p. 106 that in the tradition which the Yahwist was recording, the original state of the universe before the process of creation was very different from that depicted in the Priestly writer's source. It may be pointed out here that neither of these accounts is concerned with the problem which the modern mind has to face, namely, the problem of an absolute beginning, creation *ex nihilo*. They both assume the existence of some kind of material world, and deal with the question of how the ordered universe in which it was possible to live came into existence. In both these accounts the act of creation consisted in bringing order out of chaos, not of bringing matter into existence out of nothing.

In the Yahwist's tradition, the original state of the scene

of the Creator's activity was an uninhabited waste, un-tilled by man, and without rain, or the vegetation which rain produced. This is a very different picture from that presented in the Priestly writers' source. There the primeval state of the universe is a watery chaos, as it is in the Egyptian and Babylonian myths. The J–E account begins, 'In the day when Yahweh God made earth and heaven (and) no plant of the field was yet in the earth, and no herb of the field had yet sprung up: for Yahweh God had not caused it to rain upon the earth, and there was not a man to till the ground . . .' The whole of this sentence is a temporal clause introducing the first act of Yahweh. It is clear that the P description of a watery chaos represents the point of view of the Mesopotamian myth, but the tradition followed by the Yahwist represents the scene of Yahweh's creative activities as a soil (*'adāmah*), potentially fertile, but waste and barren until Yahweh has brought rain to fertilize it and made man to till it. Both the Nile valley and the Tigris–Euphrates delta were dependent upon irrigation from the rivers for their fertility, but cultivation in Palestine has always depended upon the regular autumn and spring rains which were regarded as the special gift of Yahweh (cf. Jer. 5:24; 14:22; Deut. 11:9–12, *et al.*). Hence the background here is not Mesopotamian or Egyptian, but Palestinian, and represents the early Canaanite idea of how life and cultivation in Canaan first came into being. But before the sending of rain from Yahweh, which is implied in verse 5, a mysterious event took place which is not attributed to the act of Yahweh. In verse 9 it is said that something came up from the earth and soaked the surface of the ground (*'adāmah*, the soil). Both the Authorized Version and Revised Version render the Hebrew word *'ēd* as 'mist'; the only other occurrence of the word is in Job 36:27, and its meaning is very uncertain. The versions suggest the mean-

ing 'fountain', or 'spring', something breaking up from
the depths of the earth, and some such meaning is more
suitable to the context here. The suggestion is that the soil
is soaked by some unexplained outbreak of water, and thus
prepared for the first creative act. Yahweh proceeds to
mould man out of the moist earth, like a potter. The Hebrew
word used here for 'made' is not the word used in the P
account (1 : 27), but is the regular word used for the potter's
operations. In the various Mesopotamian myths of creation
the making of man is depicted as a magical operation by
which some of the gods in consultation fashion man out of
clay to be the servant of the gods. In the Babylonian Epic
of Creation, after his conquest of the monster Tiamat, the
god Marduk makes man out of clay mixed with the blood
of the god Kingu. In the Yahwist's source the blood of
the god as the vital principle is replaced by the divine
breath; Yahweh breathes into man's nostrils 'breath of life'.
The idea of the creation of man as the act of a divine potter
is also found in the Egyptian myth, where the god Khnum
is depicted as forming the first man and woman on a potter's wheel (p. 73). But the source of the Palestinian myth
which the Yahwist is using is probably Mesopotamian, as
other details of the story suggest.

Then, out of the same soil, Yahweh causes trees of
various kinds to grow, and in the original form of verse 15
he assigns to the man whom he has fashioned out of the
soil the task of tilling and caring for the soil. The Hebrew
form of verse 15 shows that the Yahwist has introduced an
element of the Paradise story into a context to which it
does not belong, as we shall see farther on.

Next, and again out of the soil, Yahweh moulds animals
and birds, to see if they may provide a help for the man,
but since the man recognizes none of these as suitable for
this purpose, Yahweh causes a magic sleep (the Hebrew

word *tardēmah* indicates a supernatural sleep; compare Gen. 15:12) to overwhelm the man, and takes out a 'rib' (the Hebrew word also means 'side') and 'builds' it into a woman. When the man awakes from his supernatural slumber he recognizes the woman as his counterpart, and in 3:20 gives her the name *Hawwah*, Eve, which means 'life'. The other appellation given to her in 2:3, *'Ishshah*, is not a proper name but the usual Hebrew word for 'wife', the feminine of *'ish*, man, or husband (cf. Hos. 2:16).

This is the outline of the ancient Palestinian myth of creation which the Yahwist has used in the construction of his narrative. Now we find that he has woven into this myth with its Palestinian colouring another myth with an entirely different background, the myth of Paradise. This element is first introduced in 2:8, where it is said that Yahweh 'planted a garden in Eden, to the east'; in verse 9b the two mythical trees are brought into the story; in verse 15 the garden of Eden has been inserted in place of the original 'soil', and in verses 16–17 we have the prohibition against eating of the fruit of the tree which is in the midst of the garden. In the original form of the prohibition the nature of the tree was probably not disclosed. Then follows, in Chapter 3, the story of 'man's first disobedience', the guile of the serpent, the eating of the fruit of the tree and its consequences, and the expulsion of the guilty pair from the garden lest they should eat of the tree of life and become immortal like the gods. Many scholars hold that the semi-mythical geography of Paradise in 2:10–14 does not belong to the Yahwist's narrative but is an editorial gloss containing very ancient ideas about the location of Paradise.

Now, even apart from these verses in which the Mesopotamian colouring is very clear, we can see that the background of the Paradise myth is not that of the Palestinian myth of Creation which the Yahwist has used to form part of his narrative. The place where Yahweh has planted the garden lies away in the east, in a region called Eden. There is, certainly, a locality called Eden which is mentioned several times in the Old Testament (2 Kings 19:12, Ezek. 27:23; Amos 1:5), but the Eden of this ancient myth belongs rather to 'the land east of the sun, west of the moon', than to any geographical locality. The Akkadian word *edinu* means 'plain' or 'steppe', and it has been plausibly suggested that the garden was conceived of as springing magically out of the sandy wastes of the waterless steppe. It is possible that the Yahwist may have had in mind a contrast between the well-watered soil of his own land (cf. Deut. 8:7) and the desert where the Bedouin wandered, a place where only a miracle of divine power could create a garden. The thought of Yahweh's power as causing an Eden to arise in the wilderness is a favourite one with the prophets (cf. Isa. 41:19; 51:3).

Another form of the Paradise myth is to be found in Ezek. 28:12–19 containing features which do not appear in the Genesis form of the myth. The allusions are not all intelligible to us now, but the garden is in the mountain of the gods, a concept which occurs in the Ugaritic myths; the king-god of Tyre has his dwelling there, and is described as 'the covering cherub', and as 'walking up and down in the midst of the stones of fire'; music is there, and in the end this inhabitant of the garden of the gods is cast out as profane. The idea of the dweller in the garden as the embodiment of wisdom is referred to in Job 15:7–8, where the first man is described as the possessor of wisdom and as having heard the secret counsel of God.

Hence it seems clear that the Yahwist is using for his own purpose a myth which formed part of ancient Hebrew tradition, and something must be said about the source of the myth and the way in which the Yahwist has used it.

Recent Sumerian studies [5] have shown that the conception of a divine garden and of a state when sickness and death did not exist and wild animals did not prey on one another is to be found in Sumerian mythology. The description of this earthly Paradise is contained in the Sumerian poem which Dr Kramer has called the Epic of Emmerkar:

> The land Dilmun is a pure place, the land Dilmun is a clean
>> place,
> The land Dilmun is a clean place, the land Dilmun is a bright
>> place.
> In Dilmun the raven uttered no cry,
> The kite uttered not the cry of the kite,
> The lion killed not,
> The wolf snatched not the lamb,
> Unknown was the kid-killing dog,
> Unknown was the grain-devouring boar ...
> The sick-eyed says not 'I am sick-eyed',
> The sick-headed says not 'I am sick-headed',
> Its (Dilmun's) old woman says not 'I am an old woman',
> Its old man says not 'I am an old man',
> Unbathed is the maid, no sparkling water is poured in the city,
> Who crosses the river (of death?) utters no ...
> The wailing priests walk not about him,
> The singer utters no wail,
> By the side of the city he utters no lament.

Later, in the Semitic editing of the Sumerian myths, Dilmun became the dwelling of the immortals, where Utnapishtim and his wife were allowed to live after the Flood (p. 49). It was apparently located at the mouth of the Persian Gulf.

According to the Sumerian myth the only thing which Dilmun lacked was fresh water; the god Enki (or Ea) ordered Utu, the sun-god, to bring up fresh water from the earth to water the garden. Here we may have the source of the mysterious *'ēd* of which the Yahwist speaks as coming up from the ground to water the garden.

In the myth of Enki and Ninhursag it is related that the mother-goddess Ninhursag caused eight plants to grow in the garden of the gods. Enki desired to eat these plants and sent his messenger Isimud to fetch them. Enki ate them one by one, and Ninhursag in her rage pronounced the curse of death upon Enki. As the result of the curse eight of Enki's bodily organs were attacked by disease and he was at the point of death. The great gods were in dismay and Enlil was powerless to help. Ninhursag was induced to return and deal with the situation. She created eight goddesses of healing who proceeded to heal each of the diseased parts of Enki's body. One of these parts was the god's rib, and the goddess who was created to deal with the rib was named Ninti, which means 'the lady of the rib'. But the Sumerian word *ti* has the double meaning of 'life' as well as 'rib', so that Ninti could also mean 'the lady of life'. We have seen that in the Hebrew myth the woman who was fashioned from Adam's rib was named by him *Hawwah*, meaning 'Life'. Hence one of the most curious features of the Hebrew myth of Paradise clearly has its origin in this somewhat crude Sumerian myth.

Other elements in the Yahwist's form of the Paradise myth have striking parallels in various Akkadian myths. The importance of the possession of knowledge, which is always magical knowledge, is a recurring theme. We have seen that the myth of Adapa and the Gilgamesh Epic are both concerned with the search for immortality and the problem of death and the existence of disease. These and other examples which we have cited will serve to illustrate the point that the Akkadian myths were concerned with the themes which appear in the Yahwist's Paradise story. The inhabitants of the Tigris–Euphrates valley were confronted by various natural phenomena. There were the destructive floods, the necessity of unremitting labour in the fields in order to wring from the reluctant soil the means of subsistence, there was the mystery of childbirth, the mystery of life and death, disease and pain, and the secret ways of the serpent. Hence nothing was so important as to have knowledge about these things, not in order to satisfy curiosity about origins, but in order to control or propitiate the mysterious powers behind these things. Knowledge of good and evil was not moral knowledge, but the knowledge of friendly and hostile forces, the knowledge of powerful incantations and rituals by which these forces might be controlled. But, as we have seen, the various rituals had their spoken part, the myth, which possessed the same magic potency as the action which it accompanied and described. This was the source of the myths of Paradise, Creation, the Flood, and other similar material, which had passed into the traditions of peoples who had come under the influence of Mesopotamian culture. This material which the Yahwist found existing among the traditions of his own people he took and wove into a story embodying his own beliefs about the relation between God and man, beliefs which underlie the ancient dress which the Yahwist has so skilfully preserved.

Before we examine the Priestly version of the myth of Creation it is desirable that we should consider what the Hebrew writer whom we call the Yahwist has done with the myths which we have described. Already, as the result of the settlement of Semitic peoples in Mesopotamia, the ancient and crude Sumerian myths had undergone a process of editorial revision. If we compare the Babylonian Epic of Creation with the Sumerian myths it is apparent that many of the cruder elements have been suppressed, and a greater degree of literary skill is manifest. But as the Semitic settlers had adopted or already possessed the same general ideas about the nature of the universe as their Sumerian predecessors, there was no fundamental change in the myths. When, however, we consider the revision and reshaping which the myths have undergone at the hand of the Hebrew writer, we discover that an essential change has taken place. His treatment of the traditional material is governed by a conception wholly absent from the outlook of those who composed or transmitted the ancient myths. Looking back over the history of Israel he sees in it an intelligent design in which the activities of a God, who is a moral being, all-powerful and all-wise, are discernible. The design begins with Creation and the writer traces its course through the divine choice of his own people Israel as the instrument of that design, on to a future whose outcome is expressed in terms of myth, as the beginning was. The Yahwist is writing what has been felicitously called *Heilsgeschichte*, 'salvation-history'. Later Hebrew writers often insist on the fact that there was no human witness to the divine act of Creation. The author of the book of Job represents Yahweh as ironically asking Job, 'Where wast thou when I laid the foundations of the earth?' (Job 38:4). Hence the only way in which the beginning and the end of that 'salvation-history' which the Hebrew writer is recording could be expressed is in terms of myth. The images and symbols of the myth, the slaying of the dragon, the garden, the tree of the knowledge of good and evil, the serpent, all become the language in which to express that which could not be expressed in any other way. The other myths in Gen. 1–11 which we have yet to examine, episodical and isolated in their original setting, become woven into a continuous narrative whose theme is the development of a divine purpose.

The P Version. When, after the return of a small body of

exiles from Babylon as the result of the liberal policy of Cyrus, the Temple of Jerusalem was rebuilt and the cult restored, a class of priestly persons called scribes, of whom Ezra, the priest and scribe, is the prototype, began to concern themselves with the legal and historical traditions of their people. We know, both from the evidence of later Jewish literature and from internal evidence, that it was the labours of these pious and learned men which gave to the literature of Israel the form in which we have it now, the collection of books which we call the Old Testament. There can be little doubt that among the documents of which they made use in their task of compiling the records of Israel they possessed the account of the early history of mankind and of the ancestors of the Hebrews in the form which had been given to it by the Yahwist and the Elohist. The separate narratives of J and E had already been combined (according to the Documentary hypothesis), and had passed through several stages of editing. The Priestly editor has left the Yahwist's story of Creation and Paradise practically untouched, so that we may infer that he agreed with the account as he found it there and accepted its religious point of view. But he has prefixed to the J account of Creation another account which, as we have already seen, differs from the J account in a number of important particulars. Hence we have to inquire, as we did in the case of the J account, what sources underlie the Priestly account, what is the religious point of P, and why he thought it necessary to prefix a second account of Creation to the J account.

The break between the P and the J–E traditions occurs in the middle of 2:4. The P account ends with the words which sum up the divine act previously described, 'These are the generations (Hebrew tol^edoth) of the heaven and of the earth when they were created.' We have already seen that in both the Egyptian and the Babylonian myths the activity of creation consists in a process of begetting. The opening lines of the Akkadian Epic of Creation contain a genealogical table (p. 42) handed on from the earlier Sumerian form of the myth. The notion that creation consisted in an act of procreation has survived in the P account, in the word 'generations', but has entirely lost its original meaning; it has been demythologized.

We have already seen that the general background of the J account is Mesopotamian, although there is a strong Palestinian colouring which suggests that the Mesopotamian material had been absorbed by Canaanite culture before it was used by the Hebrew writer. It has long been recognized that there is a general resemblance between the account of the Creation contained in the Babylonian Epic of Creation and the account given by the Priestly writer. In contrast to the waterless waste which is J's description of the original state of things before Yahweh's creative activities began, the primeval condition of the universe in P's account is a disordered chaos of waters, a state which closely corresponds with the description of the primeval state given in both the Sumerian and the Babylonian forms of the Creation myth.

Moreover, the Hebrew word used for the chaos of waters, 'the deep', is *tᵉhôm*, a word which is generally acknowledged to be a Hebrew corruption of the name *Tiamat*, the Babylonian name of the chaos-dragon slain by Marduk before he proceeded to create order out of chaos. We saw (p. 45) that in the *Enuma elish* Marduk splits Tiamat's body in two and fixes half of it in the heavens to keep the waters above in their place. This corresponds to the P account of the creation of the firmament, which is depicted as a solid vault stretched out above the earth (cf. Job 38:4–11).

There is also a general resemblance to the Babylonian order of Creation in the P account of the successive acts of

Creation on the six days. Hence, in spite of the complete transformation of the Babylonian material effected by the Priestly writer, it is difficult to avoid the conclusion that the original form of the Creation story upon which he is depending is ultimately of Babylonian origin, unmodified, as was J–E's material, by Canaanite influence.

But we have still to deal with the question why the Priestly writer prefixed a second account to that which he found in the Yahwist's document, and why the Priestly account is arranged in the formal order of seven days.

It should be recalled that the members of the school or guild of scribes to which Ezra belonged were priests. Their interest centred in the Temple and the cult. Their attitude towards the material with which they were dealing was liturgical rather than historical. It was they who assigned the Psalms to their proper use at the great festivals of the Hebrew sacred year; they also originated the arrangement of the Pentateuch and the rest of the Old Testament in sections for use in public worship. They were specially concerned to preserve and revise the order of the traditional seasonal festivals. Now the researches of scholars in recent years have made it clear that from a very early period the Hebrews had been accustomed to celebrate a New Year Festival whose main outlines bore some resemblance to the great New Year Festival which had been celebrated in the cities of Mesopotamia from ancient times. One of the features of this festival was the enthronement of the king as the representative of the god, Ashur or Marduk, accompanied by the re-enactment of the god's victory over Tiamat, and the chanting of a hymn of praise to Marduk under his fifty divine names. In Babylon, the Epic of Creation had a special place in these ceremonies, and it was chanted as a magic incantation of life-giving power at the point in the ritual where the god returned to life.

Recent studies have suggested that the Hebrew New Year Festival had features in common with the Babylonian festival, and that the enthronement of Yahweh and the celebration of his mighty acts formed the central feature of the ritual. We have already seen that Hebrew poetry has preserved the myth of Yahweh's slaying the chaos-dragon, and that the references to Creation in Ps. 104 show a dependence on the P account of the Creation. It is also to be observed that this account has the form not of a narrative like the J account, but of a strophical arrangement with a repeated refrain. Its form and arrangement suggest a liturgical purpose. Moreover, we know that the Hebrew New Year Festival was celebrated for seven days, a fact which provides an intelligible explanation for the arrangement of the acts of Creation in a series of seven periods. Hence it is suggested that the sections of the J account of Creation were read by the priests at the New Year Festival, and that Gen. 1–2:4a constituted a liturgy of creation which was chanted by the priests on that occasion, and that its natural place in the roll which would be used in the New Year liturgy would be at the beginning of the whole section dealing with Yahweh's creative activities.

THE MYTH OF CAIN AND ABEL

We have already pointed out that the purpose for which the Yahwist has collected a group of myths belonging to the tradition of his people and arranged them in the form of a continuous narrative was to present the history of mankind and of his own people Israel as 'salvation-history'. The order which Yahweh had established in the act of Creation had been thrown back into chaos by man's disobedience, and the Hebrew writer has set himself the task of recording, on the one hand the disastrous consequences of man's breach of the relationship established at Creation between himself and the Creator, and on the other the persistent activity of Yahweh directed towards the restoration of that which had been destroyed. With this end in view the Yahwist has selected a myth which depicts the first consequence of the original disaster, namely, the breakdown of the family relationship, brother slaying brother.

It is clear, when the story is analysed, that the episode of Cain and Abel belongs to a different source and comes from a different cycle of ancient tradition from that whence the myths of Creation and the garden of Eden were drawn. It is easy to see that the myth of Cain and Abel is artificially linked up with the myth of Paradise, and that the Yahwist has brought together unrelated strands of tradition in the myth itself.

In the Yahwist's story, Cain and Abel are the children of Adam and Eve, born after the expulsion from Eden. Cain is represented as an agriculturalist and his brother as a pastoralist. The brothers bring offerings to Yahweh. Cain brings the fruits of his labour on the soil, and Abel brings firstlings from his flock. Cain's offering is rejected, while his brother's is accepted. In anger at the rejection of his own offering and jealousy because of the acceptance of his brother's, Cain kills his brother. The myth goes on to relate the curse pronounced upon Cain by Yahweh, his flight from the scene of the slaying, and the protective mark placed upon him by Yahweh. Cain then settles in the land of Nod, builds a city, and becomes the ancestor of descendants to whom the origins of civilization are attributed.

A careful examination of the myth in the form in which it appears in the Biblical narrative shows that it is made up of various strands of myth and saga which were originally distinct, and none of which had any connexion with the Paradise myth. In the setting in which the Yahwist has placed the episode, Adam and Eve, Cain and Abel, are the only living persons in existence. But the myth supposes that Cain goes in fear of human vengeance; he says, 'Every one that findeth me shall slay me.' The ritual of sacrifice is assumed, and a stage of civilization has been reached which implies the building of cities and a knowledge of metalworking and the construction of musical instruments. All this is quite incompatible with the beginnings of life upon the earth after the expulsion from Paradise. Analysis of the myth reveals that three different strands of tradition have been woven together, either by the Yahwist, or in the sources which he is using.

(a) The first of these strands reflects the ancient feud between the desert and the sown land, between the settled tiller of the soil and the pastoral nomad. We have already seen that this theme is the subject of the Sumerian myth of Dumuzi and Enkimdu (p. 35), where Dumuzi the shepherd-god and the Enkimdu the farmer-god contend with offerings for the favour of Ishtar. In this form of the myth, however, there is no tragic ending.

(b) The second strand contains the outline of a ritual myth which has been much worked over. It has no connexion with the Paradise myth, but implies a developed stage of society, with established religious institutions. Cain and Abel represent two different types of community, each carrying out its regular ritual of sacrifice. The rejection of the agriculturist's offering implies a failure of crops, and this calls for some form of expiatory ritual. The necessity for such a ritual explains the obscure conversation between Cain and Yahweh in 4:6–7. The Hebrew text has suffered considerable corruption in the course of transmission. Its form seems to suggest that the agriculturalist, whose sacrifice has failed to secure its object, has consulted the oracle to inquire what is to be done, and has received a reply saying that he knows what the proper ritual is, and that there is a *rōbēs*, a hostile demonic power waiting to be propitiated. The word translated 'lieth' or 'croucheth' is the same as the Akkadian *rabisu*, 'the evil croucher', who lies in wait for his offering, and is frequently mentioned in Babylonian magical texts.

The next step is introduced by a significant phrase which is omitted in the Hebrew text but is supplied by the Septuagint, and is given in the Revised Version margin. It says, 'And Cain said unto Abel his brother, Let us go into the field.' This detail is also found in the Sumerian myth just referred to, where the farmer-god invites the shepherd-god to bring his sheep and let them pasture in his, the farmer-god's, fields. It is in the *field*, the tilled soil, whose infertility has brought about the situation, that the slaying of the shepherd takes place, and the suggestion is that the slaying was a ritual one; it was not an impulsive one instigated by jealousy, but a communal ritual killing intended to fertilize the soil by drenching it with the blood of the victim; in the words of the narrative, 'the earth has opened her mouth to receive thy brother's blood.'

Then follows the curse of Cain, his flight from the scene of the slaying, and the protective mark which he receives from Yahweh. Here there are obvious difficulties. Yahweh curses the slayer and at the same time places him under his protection; also the nature of the mark has been the source of much speculation. Sir James Frazer has suggested that God may have decorated Cain with red, black, or white paint, or perhaps with a tasteful combination of these colours, after the manner of various savage peoples. He concludes his study of the myth with the following humorous remarks, 'Thus adorned, the first Mr Smith – for Cain means Smith – may have paraded the waste places of the earth without the least fear of being recognized and molested by his victim's ghost. This explanation of the mark of Cain has the advantage of relieving the Biblical narrative from a manifest absurdity. For on the usual interpretation God affixed the mark to Cain in order to save him from human assailants, apparently forgetting that there was nobody to assail him, since the earth was as yet inhabited only by the murderer and his parents. Hence by assuming that the foe of whom the first murderer went in fear was a ghost instead of a living man, we avoid the irreverence of imputing to the deity a grave lapse of memory little in keeping with the divine omniscience.' [6]

Ingenious as this explanation is, a better explanation of this feature of the myth is to be found in parallels provided by certain seasonal rituals such as the Babylonian New Year Festival, or the Athenian ritual of the Bouphonia. [7]

In the Babylonian New Year Festival, whose purpose was wholly agricultural, a sacrificing priest and an exorcist purified the shrine of the god Nabu, Marduk's son, with the carcase of a slain sheep, smearing the walls of the shrine with the blood of the sheep; after this they were obliged to flee into the desert until the festival was over because they were defiled by their ritual act. [8] In the Hebrew ritual of the Day of Atonement, originally part of the autumn New Year Festival, we find a similar combination of a ritual slaying and a flight, but here the human participants in the ritual are replaced by animal victims, namely, two goats, one of which is slain while the other is driven out into the desert. [9] Again, in the Athenian ritual of the Bouphonia, an ox was ritually slaughtered by two men who were then obliged to flee.

Hence it is suggested that the flight of Cain originally represented a ritual flight. The sacrificer was defiled by his act and was driven out by the community until he had been purified; his guilt was a communal and not an individual guilt. This explains why the slayer enjoyed ritual protection. He was no common murderer, but a priest or sacred person who had performed an act for the benefit of the community; an act which involved ceremonial defilement and the consequent temporary banishment of the slayer; but his person was sacrosanct. Moreover, the most probable explanation of the mark is that it represented a tattoo mark or other indication that the fugitive belonged to a sacred class. We have evidence from the Old Testament that the prophets bore such marks,[10] and the existence of such marks to distinguish the members of temple staffs as the property of the god is abundantly attested in ancient literature.

Thus the original form of the first part of the Yahwist's story of Cain and Abel, namely, that contained in 4:1–15, was probably a ritual myth depicting a ritual slaying intended to secure fertility for the crops; the slaying was followed by the flight of the slayer, who was protected by a mark which indicated his sacred character.

But, like other myths, before it was used by the Yahwist for his own religious purposes it had in the course of transmission acquired other meanings and uses. It had come to represent the feud between the settled peasant, tilling his fields, and the pastoral, half-nomad peoples who lived on the borders of the settled fertile lands, and were continually attempting to enter them. The myth has also acquired an aetiological character as an explanation of the origin of the blood-feud. The suggestion sometimes put forward that the myth is intended to explain Yahweh's preference for animal sacrifices is not satisfactory, since, in the Levitical sacrificial code, such a preference does not appear, but both animal and vegetable offerings have their appointed place.

The second part of the myth, which, in its present form

continues the adventures of Cain, is from an entirely different source, and represents a totally distinct tradition. It is most probably a fragment of the early tradition of the Kenite clan, of whom we are told various details in the history of the Hebrews. But it would also appear that the fragment of Kenite tradition which forms the nucleus of the second part of the Cain and Abel myth has become mixed with other elements foreign to the Kenite tradition. The Kenites were always nomads or half-nomads, tent-dwellers,[11] but the ancestor of the Kenite clan is depicted in this part of the myth as a city-builder, a settled inhabitant of a land which cannot be identified geographically. He is represented as the founder of a line from whence spring the various elements of civilized life. When we compare the genealogy of Cain given by the Yahwist in 4:17–18 with the Priestly genealogy of Seth given in 5:1–30 it is clear that the two genealogies are parallel forms of the same tradition about the descendants of the first man. This may best be seen if the two are placed side by side:

	J	P
1	Adam	Adam
2	—	Seth
3	—	Enosh
4	Cain	Kenan
5	Enoch	Mahalalel
6	Irad	Jared
7	Mehujael	Enoch
8	Methushael	Methulselah
9	Lamech	Lamech
10	—	Noah

If these two lists are compared it will be seen how close is the parallel between them. First, the father of Kenan in P's list is Enosh; but this is merely another Hebrew word for 'man' and a synonym for Adam, the first man. Kenan is another Hebrew form of Cain, so that in the original form of both lists the first man was the father of Cain. Then Irad is the same as Jared; Enoch occurs in both lists; for Mehujael the Septuagint has Maleleel, i.e., Mahalalel, and for Methushael it has Mathusala, i.e., Methuselah; and, finally, Lamech occurs in both lists. Hence it cannot be doubted that we have two different versions of the same list, and that J's list of Cain's descendants is really the genealogy of the first inhabitants of the earth, and the second part of the myth is really the account of the origin of the various elements of early civilization.

We have, therefore, three distinct elements which the Yahwist either wove together into a connected narrative and linked up with the Paradise story, or found already brought together in traditions of the Kenite clan and made use of for his special religious purpose. The long-standing connexion of the Kenites with the Hebrews goes back to the saga of Moses, who is represented as having married into the Kenite clan (cf. Judges 4:11 where 'brother-in-law' should be 'father-in-law', as in Revised Version margin), and this may explain why the Yahwist could find and make use of Kenite traditions in his story of the origins of Israel. It may be added that the fragment of ancient poetry preserved in 4:23–4 where the desert code of blood revenge is greatly intensified and referred back to the ancestor of the Kenites, supports the view that it was from Kenite traditions that the Yahwist drew the material for this part of his story. The three elements thus preserved, transformed, and woven into a continuous narrative, are: first a ritual myth describing a ritual slaying and the subsequent ritual banishment; second, an aetiological myth explaining the origin of the blood-feud practised by a nomad community; and third, an ancient genealogical list embodying one of many traditions concerning the origin of civilization among the early Semites. This myth of Cain and Abel illustrates the transformations which an ancient myth, such as the Sumerian myth of the farmer and the shepherd, may undergo in the course of its wanderings.

The next myth which the Yahwist has woven into his 'salvation-history' is perhaps the most widely distributed of all myths, the myth of the Flood. We have already discussed the forms of this myth current among the Sumerians and their Semitic conquerors, and have observed that the Egyptians had no Flood myth, although they had a myth of the destruction of mankind. We shall also see that the Flood myth was not the only form of the myth of the destruction of mankind known to the Hebrew writers. But before we deal with the Hebrew form of the Flood myth there is some important mythological material to be noticed which has been used to make a narrative link between the myth of Cain and Abel and the Flood myth.

We have already pointed out that the genealogical list of ten generations from Adam to Noah is a variant version of the Yahwist's list of Cain's descendants given in Chapter 4. But there are two features of P's list which call for comment. We have seen that P is using what is commonly called the J–E narrative in his final edition of Genesis in its present form, and that he has added certain elements of his own to it. Here he has added to the J story of Cain and Abel a genealogical list which contains ten names instead of the eight names of the J list, and has assigned to the ten names an extraordinary duration of life; with the remarkable exception of Enoch, the length of life assigned to each member of P's list extends to little short of a thousand years. For the explanation of this we have to turn to those early Sumerian sources which were known to the editors of the Creation myths of the Hebrews.

A Babylonian priest named Berosus, who lived in the

reign of Alexander the Great, wrote in very bad Greek an account of the ancient traditions of Babylon, and it has been established by recent discoveries that Berosus was using ancient Sumerian king-lists.[12] Two king-lists from the Sumerian city of Larsa have been discovered, one of which contains eight names, and the other ten, and both of them conclude with the name of Ziusudra, also called in the Akkadian version Utnapishtim, the hero of the Flood myth. Both in Berosus and in the Larsa lists the prediluvian kings are said to have reigned an incredible number of years, ranging from twenty to seventy thousand years. At the end of one of the Larsa lists the scribe has appended a note which says, 'The Flood came. After the Flood came, kingship was sent down from on high.' Since Ziusudra and his wife had been made immortal and translated to Dilmun, no legitimate successor was available and, as it was not conceivable that ordered life could continue without kingship, it had to be sent down from heaven. It is possible that astrological or cult reasons may underlie these strange figures, but the explanation does not concern us here. What does concern us is the relation between the Sumerian king-lists and the genealogical list in Gen. 5. In the first place, we have in each case a list of ten names before the Flood; secondly, there is the abnormal length of life attributed to the individuals in each list; thirdly, the seventh person in each list is noteworthy for similar qualities. The seventh king in the Sumerian tradition was regarded as possessing special wisdom in matters pertaining to the gods, and as being the first of mankind to practise divination. The seventh name in the P list is that of Enoch, of whom it is said that 'he walked with God', and who in later Jewish tradition was said to have been taken up into heaven without dying.[13] It may be merely coincidence that one of the Larsa lists contains eight names and the other ten, just as the J list has eight, and the P list ten names. But the other parallels are too striking to be fortuitous. It seems difficult to avoid the inference that the Priestly writer has prefixed to his account of the Flood a list of ten patriarchs with abnormal length of life because, by the time he wrote, this element of Babylonian mythology had been absorbed into the traditions of his own people.

It has been conjectured [14] that the enormous numbers in the Sumerian king-lists may be the product of astrological speculation, a feature wholly absent from Hebrew thought until we come to the late apocalyptic literature. But the probable reason for the introduction of such numbers into the Priestly genealogy is that they are intended to correspond with the Priestly chronology which assigned a fixed number of years from the Creation to the foundation of Solomon's Temple, and divided this period into epochs, the first of which, from the Creation to the Flood, contained 1,656 years.

In the Babylonian myth of the Flood the gods decided to destroy mankind for the rather absurd reason that they had become so noisy that they prevented the gods from sleeping at nights; [15] no moral cause for this arbitrary act entered the minds of the early myth-makers. But to the Hebrew writer the myth of the Flood, fixed in the traditions of his people, as various poetic and prophetic references show, had become an awful portent, the final catastrophe brought about by man's rebellion against God. It has become an episode in the 'salvation-history', because a remnant was spared to carry on the divine purpose of ultimate restoration. This is the reason why further mythical material is introduced as a prelude to the Flood myth, in order to show how completely corrupt mankind had become. In 6:1–4 we have a fragment of mythical material, originally unconnected with the myth of the Flood, but used by the Yahwist to explain the increasing lawlessness and violence of man-kind which finally decided Yahweh to destroy the race. The myth of the union between divine and mortal beings, resulting in the birth of demi-gods or heroes, is found in the early Sumerian and Babylonian sources whose influence on Canaanite mythology appears in the Ugaritic texts. We have already observed its influence on the Hebrew myths of Creation, and Greek mythology bears witness to its wide diffusion at an early date.

Behind the brief and probably intentionally obscure reference in 6:1–4, there lies a more widely known myth of a race of semi-divine beings who rebelled against the gods and were cast down into the underworld. The beings called Nephilim in verse 4, and rendered 'giants' in the Septuagint and Authorized Version, seem to have been re-garded by the Yahwist as the offspring of the union between the 'sons of God' and the daughters of men mentioned in verse 1. The assembly of lesser gods so often referred to in Sumerian, Babylonian, and Ugaritic myths, has been trans-formed in Hebrew myth and poetry into the 'sons of God' conceived of as a kind of heavenly council over which Yahweh presided. Compare, for instance, the scene in the first chapter of Job, where the sons of God come to present themselves before Yahweh (Job 1:6). Traces of the myth are to be found in Num. 13:33 where the Nephilim are represented as the survivors of a race of giants whom the Hebrews found in Canaan when they came to settle there. Another possible reference occurs in Ezek. 32:27, where a slight emendation gives us an allusion to the Nephilim. In apocalyptic literature and in the New Testament (2 Pet. 2:4; Jude 6) the myth has been still further transformed into the myth of the fall of the angels, so splendidly por-trayed by Milton. The fragment of the myth here preserved by the Yahwist was originally an aetiological myth explaining the belief in the existence of a vanished race of giants, but the Yahwist has made use of it here to support his account of the progressive deterioration of the human race, and goes on to connect it with Yahweh's purpose to destroy man from the face of the earth.

THE MYTH OF THE FLOOD

We have already seen that more than one version of the Creation myth existed among the early traditions of Israel; the same is true of the Flood myth. In the form in which we have it in Genesis, two versions of the story have been woven together by the final editor. The second version of the myth of the destruction of mankind which also occurs in Genesis will be dealt with later. There are also references to the Flood myth in Hebrew poetry and in the prophetic writings.

The points of resemblance and difference between the Yahwist's version and that of the Priestly writer, and the dependence of both on Mesopotamian sources will be seen best if they are set out in tabular form :

SUMERIAN	BABYLONIAN	YAHWIST	PRIESTLY
Enlil decrees destruction of mankind because of their noise	Gods decree flood	Yahweh decrees destruction of man for his wickedness	Elohim decrees destruction of all flesh for its corruption
Nintu (Ishtar) protests	Ishtar protests		
Ziusudra (Akkadian Atrakhasis) hero of Flood	Utnapishtim hero of Flood	Noah hero of Flood	Noah hero of Flood

Middle Eastern Mythology

SUMERIAN	BABYLONIAN	YAHWIST	PRIESTLY
Ziusudra's piety		Noah finds favour with Yahweh	Noah only righteous man before Elohim
Ziusudra warned by Enki (Ea) in dream (by Ea through reed hut)	Utnapishtim warned by Ea through wall of reed hut		Noah warned by Elohim
Ziusudra's vessel a huge ship	Ship a cube: 120 by 120 by 120; 7 stories; 9 divisions		Ark: 300 by 50 by 50; 3 stories
		Instruction to enter ark	
	All kinds of animals	7 pairs of clean, 2 of unclean animals	2 of all animals
		Yahweh shuts Noah in	
Flood and storm	Flood from heavy rain and storm	Flood from rain	Fountains of great deep broken up, and windows of heaven opened
			Exact date of beginning and end of Flood given
Flood lasts 7 days	Flood lasts 6 days	Flood lasts 40 days, retires after 2 (3?) periods of 7 days	Flood lasts 150 days, retires in 150 days
	Ship grounds on Mt Nisir		Ark grounds on Mt Ararat

SUMERIAN	BABYLONIAN	YAHWIST	PRIESTLY
	Utnapishtim sends out dove, swallow, and raven	Noah sends out raven and dove	
Ziusudra sacrifices to Sun-god in ship	Utnapishtim offers sacrifice on Mt Nisir	Noah offers sacrifice on altar	
	Gods gather like flies to the sacrifice	Yayweh smells sweet savour	
Immortality given to Ziusudra	Immortality and deification for Utnapishtim and his wife	Yahweh resolves not to curse the ground again for man's sake	God makes covenant with Noah not to destroy the earth again by a flood
	Ishtar's necklace of lapis-lazuli as sign of remembrance		God gives rainbow as sign of remembrance

The Mesopotamian origin of the Flood myth is clear from the above table, even apart from the remarkable resemblances between the Babylonian and the Hebrew accounts. The differences between the Yahwist and the Priestly versions of the myth suggest that the latter is using a different form of the myth from that used by the former, and that the Priestly version is closer in some respects to the Mesopotamian sources. The Flood myth is frequently mentioned in later Hebrew literature; in Ps. 29:10 Yahweh is said to have been 'enthroned' at the Flood, and in Isa. 54:9 the Flood is referred to as 'the waters of Noah', and Yahweh is represented as recalling his promise not to destroy mankind by a flood again, a promise which occurs in the

Priestly version. The measurements in the Babylonian version suggest the dimensions of a building rather than of a boat, and the somewhat doubtful theory has been advanced that in these measurements a tradition has been preserved that the staged towers called 'ziqqurats', which are a regular feature of the temple buildings in ancient Mesopotamian cities, were originally designed as places of refuge from the frequent floods in the Delta.

It is possible that the Priestly writer does not include the distinction between clean and unclean animals, nor the mention of sacrifices, in his account because he regards these institutions as originating in the time of Moses. We also find in the Priestly account the pattern which he has imposed upon the history of the human race in relation to the divine purpose. He sees that purpose revealed in three successive stages, each marked by a covenant with its characteristic sign. First the covenant with Noah, marked by the sign of the rainbow; then the covenant with Abraham, to which the sign of circumcision is attached; and lastly the covenant with Israel, of which the Sabbath is the sign. There is no trace of this arrangement in the Yahwist's narrative since he regards the worship of Yahweh and the institution of sacrifice as already existing before the Flood.

THE MYTH OF THE TOWER OF BABEL

This is the last of the myths which the editors of the Old Testament have brought together in the first eleven chapters of Genesis. The myth is set in a collection of ethnological and genealogical notices, partly from the Yahwist and partly from the Priestly writer. Together they represent ancient Hebrew traditions concerning the nations by whom Israel was surrounded, especially Assyria, Babylon, and

Egypt. While the details are confused and inaccurate, the broad outlines of the ethnology and geography correspond roughly to the arrangement of the ancient world at the dawn of Hebrew history. The sons of Japheth, the Iapetic races, are located in the Caucasus and to the north and west of Asia Minor; the sons of Ham, the Hamitic group, represented by the Egyptians and Libyans, are located in Egypt, Nubia, Ethiopia, and northern Africa; but, incorrectly included among this group from the modern standpoint, are the Canaanites and the south Arabian peoples, who belong to the Semitic group; the sons of Shem, i.e., what we now designate as the Semitic peoples, include, according to P, the Elamites, a non-Semitic people, and Lud, also non-Semitic, if it is to be identified with Lydia; in the Yahwist's version of Shem's descendants (10:24–5) the majority are listed as south Arabian peoples, and Eber's genealogy is not carried beyond his first son Peleg, whose name has no ethnic associations.

This is the setting in which the myth of the Tower of Babel is embedded. It has been thought by some modern scholars that two separate traditions underlie the present form of the myth, one relating to the building of a city, Babel, and the origin of different languages; the other a tradition about the building of a tower and the dispersion of peoples in the earth; the two being subsequently woven together by the Yahwist into a single narrative, or having been already united in the source which he was using, whether oral or written.

It is clear that the myth is independent, both of the ethnological setting in which it has been placed, and of the Flood myth. It represents the first human group as settling in the Euphrates delta, discovering the use of clay for bricks, a special feature of early Mesopotamian architecture, and building a city and a tower. In spite of its Mesopotamian colouring, the story cannot be of Babylonian origin. A Babylonian myth would not have represented the sacred 'ziqqurat', regarded by the ancient Babylonians as the bond between heaven and earth,[16] as an impious attempt to scale heaven, nor would the sacred name of Babylon, *Bab-ili*, which means 'the gate of God', have been derived from the Hebrew root *bll*, meaning 'confusion', with which it has no etymological connexion. The myth rather reflects the attitude of nomads entering the fertile plains of the Delta, beholding with wonder and dread the soaring towers of Babylonian cities, and despising the multitudes speaking all the various tongues of the ancient Near East.

In the Priestly writer's account of the spread of Noah's descendants, the dispersion of races and the rise of different languages (cf. 10:5) are regarded as the natural result of increasing population and the movements of peoples, not as the result of an act of divine judgement. Thus, while the Priestly writer has accepted the story and preserved it in the final editing of the Old Testament, agreeing, no doubt, with the religious use of it made by the Yahwist, it clearly did not form part of the source which he has used in the compilation of the ethnological notices in Chapter 10. Similarly, the story is independent of the Flood tradition, and it may be compared with the brief J fragment inserted in the Priestly genealogy in 5:29. The forward reference in Lamech's words can only be to the discovery of the vine, described as taking place after the Flood (9:20), a discovery which could hardly have been a comfort to the generation which perished in the Flood.

The use which the Yahwist makes of the myth is in keeping with his view of the nature of man and the divine activity which we have already seen exemplified in his use of the Creation and Flood myths. He recognizes that even after the catastrophe of the Flood human nature remains unchanged (cf. 8 : 21), 'the imagination of man's heart is evil from his youth', and in this myth he sees man still striving after that unattainable equality with the divine which had caused the primal fall. He sees Yahweh still supreme in power and knowledge, confounding man's petty efforts to scale heaven, and proceeds to enter upon the story of Yahweh's grace responding to one man's obedience and faith.

Thus as with most of the mythological material taken over by Hebrew writers from Mesopotamian sources, either directly or indirectly, the myth has been reshaped in such a way as to provide, in symbolic terms, a picture of the divine activities, and the relations between God and man as interpreted by the prophets of Israel.

We have seen a somewhat similar process taking place, both in the development of Egyptian religion, and in the transmission of Sumerian mythology. The earlier Egyptian form of the myth of creation was transformed by what is called the Memphite theology; and the myths of Sumer were reshaped to express the pattern of Assyrian and Babylonian religion. But in the case of Israel's use of Mesopotamian and Canaanite mythology this process of transformation was much more radical and had profounder religious implications, making a more extended treatment of Hebrew mythology necessary. The myths collected in the first eleven chapters of Genesis do not, however, exhaust the mythological material contained in Hebrew literature.

THE MYTH OF THE DESTRUCTION OF THE CITIES OF THE PLAIN

We have already seen that the wide-spread myth of the destruction of mankind had assumed different forms in Egypt, Mesopotamia, and possibly in Ugaritic mythology, if we may regard the myth of Anat's slaughter of the enemies of Baal as belonging to that category. Underlying the story in Genesis of the destruction of Sodom and Gomorrah and Lot's escape, there is clearly to be seen another form of the myth of the destruction of mankind, and one which survived into Christian eschatology.

In the form in which we have it now, the story of the destruction of Sodom and Gomorrah is a composite narrative which has been woven into the saga of Abraham. It embodies several strands of ancient Hebrew tradition, one of which reflects a myth of the destruction of mankind which is independent of the Flood myth. In the thirteenth chapter of Genesis we have an account of how Lot separated himself and his possessions from his uncle Abraham and chose what is called the 'circle' of Jordan. This district is described as 'well watered everywhere, before the Lord destroyed Sodom and Gomorrah'. It is here implied that, in the tradition which the Yahwist is using, the Dead Sea and the desolate condition of the south end of the Jordan valley were the result of an act of divine judgement which destroyed the cities of the plain, or 'circle'. According to the Yahwist's narrative the destruction was effected by a rain of fire and sulphur from heaven. The reason for the destruction is said to be the special wickedness of the inhabitants of those cities, just as the Flood is said to have been caused by the wickedness of mankind. Lot is delivered as the result of the intercession of Abraham. He is commanded by the angelic instruments of his rescue not to look back, a feature of the story which finds an echo in folklore. His wife looks back and is turned into a pillar of salt, and Lot with his two daughters are the sole survivors of the catastrophe. Then follows a tradition of the origin of two of the special rivals and enemies of Israel, Moab and Ammon. Their birth is attributed to an incestuous union between Lot and his daughters, an episode which takes place while Lot is drunk, recalling the shame and drunkenness of Noah after his escape from the Flood. In 19:31 Lot's daughters are represented as saying, 'there is not a man in the earth to come in unto us after the manner of all the earth', implying the total destruction of the rest of mankind. Hence it is clear that we have here a fragment of a myth of the destruction of mankind which is independent of the Mesopotamian sources upon which the Hebrew traditions of the Flood rest. The story of the celestial visitants and their hospitable reception by Abraham, as contrasted with the reception accorded to two of them by the men of Sodom, finds an echo in Ovid's story of the reception of Zeus and Hermes by Philemon and Baucis and its sequel in the flood which destroyed the inhospitable inhabitants of the district.

The myth is referred to several times in the writings of the prophets of Israel in terms which suggest that another form of the myth may have been current. They use the word 'overthrow' to describe the destruction of the wicked cities, a word which in Hebrew usually describes the effects of an earthquake.[17]

THE CULT MYTHS

It has already been pointed out that in the class of myths which we have called ritual myths the ritual was accompanied by a spoken or chanted element, its *muthos* or myth, which described the situation which was being enacted in the ritual. The Babylonian Epic of Creation which was chanted by the priests at the New Year Festival described a situation in which the central element was the victory of Marduk over the chaos-dragon Tiamat and its result, the achievement of creation, the bringing of order out of primeval chaos. The situation was a real one, although it

could not be described as historical; somehow, at some unknown point of time, an activity had come into play which
had produced the ordered scene which was the ancient
Babylonian's environment. This activity was described in
symbolic terms of gods and dragons, of generation, of death
and resurrection, but it could not be doubted that the symbols stood for some kind of reality.

We have seen that much of this ancient mythological
material had been taken up into the traditions of Israel, but
something was happening in Israel which was new and had
no counterpart elsewhere. A new sense of reality was coming to birth, the reality of Israel's God. Its beginnings are
shrouded in mystery; it may have begun with Abraham who
is no longer regarded by most scholars as a mythical figure,
or it may have begun with Moses, but by the time that the
Yahwist was compiling or composing the early records of
Israel, Yahweh, Israel's God, stood out like a rock against
the misty background of the surrounding polytheism. In
contrast with the shadowy figures of the Egyptian, Babylonian, or Canaanite gods, Yahweh was a real person with
a moral character, and a purpose which gave meaning to
the events of Israel's history.

One of the results of this development was the conversion of the myth to a new use. The sagas of the patriarchs
in Genesis show that tribal traditions had been preserved,
orally or in writing, from a very early period, and the sagas
of the deliverance from Egypt under Moses, the wilderness
wanderings, and the conquest of Canaan under Joshua, show
that national traditions had similarly been preserved from
an early date. When the Hebrews entered Canaan the evidence of archaeology has shown [18] that they took over
the great Canaanite cult-centres, such as Shechem, Bethel,
and Shiloh, and made them tribal or regional centres of the
cult of Yahweh. Before Solomon made Jerusalem the chief

national cult-centre, and probably long after, it was at these tribal and regional centres that the main seasonal festivals were celebrated. In Deut. 26:1–11 we have an example of the pattern of such a seasonal ritual, probably describing what happened at a local shrine at the Feast of Ingathering, later called the Feast of Tabernacles. The Israelite brought his offering and handed it over to the priest who placed it before the altar. Then followed what might be called the festal liturgy with antiphonal responses. The worshipper recited before the priest and the altar the cult myth of the Exodus and the entry into Canaan. The implication of this interesting Deuteronomic passage is that the tradition of what had happened to Israel in the remote past had been preserved by the priests in the local cult-centres, thrown into liturgical form, and imparted to successive generations of Israelites. Just as the myth of Marduk's victory over Tiamat was recited at the Babylonian New Year Festival, so at the seasonal festivals of Israel the *muthos*, the ritual recitation, of the mighty acts of Yahweh, was a central feature of such occasions. It is relevant here to point out that the prophets of Israel, who were the interpreters of Israel's past in terms of 'salvation-history', have used the mythological imagery of Babylon to describe the deliverance of Israel from Egypt by the mighty hand of Yahweh. Egypt has become the dragon smitten by Yahweh's sword (Isa. 51:9–10). This has been called the historicization of myth, but it would be more accurate to regard it as the conversion of myth to a new use. The most important of these cult myths call for some account here.

The Passover Cult Myth [19]

While it cannot be doubted that historical events underlie the narrative in Exodus of the sojourn of Israel in Egypt and their escape from it, yet the form in which the story has been transmitted is not history. The account of the ten plagues by which Pharaoh was finally forced to let Israel go, of the dividing of the Red Sea to allow Israel to pass through, of the power displayed by Moses' rod, and of the Pillar of cloud and fire in which Yahweh manifested his presence among his people, is the form in which the mighty acts of Yahweh were preserved and recited in liturgical antiphony at the cult-festival of Passover year after year in the spring. From Exod. 12 : 24–27 and 13 : 14–15 it may be seen that the myth accompanying the Passover ritual had been thrown into the form of liturgical responses, and the whole 'service', as it is here called, was designed to be the glorification of Yahweh and the memorial of his redemptive activity. While the feast may have begun as a family ritual, it soon developed into a festival celebrated at a central sanctuary, and finally could only be celebrated within the precincts of the Temple at Jerusalem. A careful examination of the details of the ten plagues will show that it is not history which is being presented here. For instance, after Moses has turned all the waters of Egypt into blood, we are told that Pharaoh's magicians did the same, which is obviously impossible since all the water in Egypt, including the Nile, had already been turned into blood. The general pattern of the Passover cult myth is repeated several times in liturgies in the Psalter, for example in Pss. 78, 105, 106, and notably in Ps. 136 where the antiphonal character of the liturgical responses is very marked, the congregation answering each utterance of the priests with the refrain 'For his mercy endureth for ever'. In these Psalms we have the cult myth preserved in its fixed liturgical form, while in Exodus it is used by the editors of the Pentateuch as the basis of the 'salvation-history' which records for Israel the redemptive activity of Yahweh.

The Myth of the Epiphany on Sinai

It has been pointed out that the cult myth which we have described above contains no reference to a most important feature of the 'salvation-history' in the Pentateuch, the epiphany of Yahweh on Sinai and the establishment of the covenant with Israel. The suggestion, which has much to commend it, has been made that, underlying the confused narrative in Exod. 19–34, we have a cult myth independent of the Paschal cult myth and attached to another important cultic occasion. We have already alluded to the fact, established by archaeological evidence, that Israel took over the Canaanite sanctuaries after their settlement in the land, and converted them to the worship of Yahweh. One of the most important of these cult-centres was Shechem, and in the twenty-fourth chapter of the book of Joshua we have an account of a gathering of all the tribes at Shechem, a recital of the Passover cult myth, and the performance of a covenant ritual at the sacred oak at Shechem, 'that was in the sanctuary of Yahweh' (24:26). We have also an account in Deut. 27 of a covenant ritual which was to be performed at the twin peaks of Ebal and Gerizim, i.e., at Shechem.

It would seem, therefore, that early in the period of the settlement a covenant festival was celebrated at Shechem at which the cult myth of the epiphany on Sinai and the giving of the Law was recited.[20] In Jos. 8:30–35 we have an account of the performance of this ritual by Joshua at Shechem in the presence of 'all Israel', and it is recorded that he read all the words of the law to the people. 'There was not a word of all that Moses commanded, which Joshua read not before all the assembly of Israel.' We are also told that one of the features of this ceremony was a solemn re-affirmation of the covenant which, according to the tradition, had been established by Yahweh with Israel at Sinai.

Middle Eastern Mythology

What actually took place at Sinai cannot be disentangled from the cult myth in which it has been embodied, neither has the exact site of Sinai ever been determined, but it is clear that all the details of the Exodus narrative, like those of the Passover myth, are intended to set forth the glory and unapproachable holiness of Yahweh. One of the prominent features of the epiphany is the myth of the Presence in the Shekinah, a myth which has been described as peculiar to Israel.[21] The beginnings of the myth are to be seen in the account in Gen. 15 of the first covenant with Abraham. After performing the very ancient ritual of the dividing of slain victims, Abraham in a trance sees Yahweh pass between the divided corpses of the victims in the form of 'a smoking furnace and a flaming torch' (Gen. 15:17). Then, at the crossing of the Red Sea, Yahweh appears in a pillar of cloud and fire and comes between Israel and their pursuers. In the cult myth of the epiphany on Sinai, Yahweh descends upon the burning mountain in a cloud and fire. This symbolic element in the myth persists throughout the history of Israel. In the oracles of Isaiah, the presence of Yahweh in Zion as a burning fire is declared by the prophet to be the protection of Jerusalem from her adversaries, as well as destruction for the ungodly (Isa. 31:9; 33:14). The most elaborate development of the myth is seen in the visions of Ezekiel. The prophet sees 'a great cloud with fire flashing continually' (Ezek. 1:4); the cloud opens to disclose the vision of the cherubim and the throne of Yahweh, and the prophet sees the whole epiphany of the glory of Yahweh leave the Temple and ultimately the city.

In the New Testament the myth of the Shekinah reappears in the Synoptic account of the Transfiguration where 'a shining cloud' overshadows the disciples (Matt. 17:5). In 1 Cor. 10:1-2 Paul tells the Corinthians that Israel had been 'baptized' unto Moses in the cloud, where the myth has become a symbol of Christian baptism.

The myth of the epiphany on Sinai, preserved at Israel's cult-centres, and recited at the festival of the renewal of the covenant, became as deeply embedded in the literary tradition of Israel as the Paschal cult legend. It recurs over and over again in the poetry of Israel. In the very ancient 'Song of Deborah', celebrating a victory over the Canaanites, and, according to some scholars, sung at a cult-festival, there is a description of the epiphany of Yahweh on Sinai. It occurs in Ps. 18:9–14, and in many other passages of Hebrew poetry.

On the Babylonian monument known as the stele of Hammurabi, the king is represented as receiving from the god Shamash the ancient collection of laws commonly called the Code of Hammurabi. The sanctity of the code was affirmed in the myth of its reception from the hand of the deity. So in the case of the early legislation of Israel, contained in Exod. 21–3, generally called the Book of the Covenant, the laws are embedded in a narrative framework which is based on the cult myth of the epiphany on Sinai. The laws are represented as inscribed on tables of stone and handed to Moses by Yahweh, thus establishing their sanctity.

We pass now to other mythical elements in the traditions of Israel. Before we do so, it may be useful to say a few words about the rationalization of the myths in Hebrew tradition. It is possible, and has often been attempted, to explain both Old and New Testament 'miracles' in terms of natural phenomena. Thus the ten plagues of Egypt have been explained as purely natural phenomena exploited by Moses to cause superstitious awe in the minds of Pharaoh and his people. The collapse of the walls of Jericho has been explained as the result of an earthquake shock which had also caused the temporary damming up of the bed of the Jordan, enabling the Israelites to pass over dry-shod. But such an approach to these episodes may cause those who adopt it to lose sight of the real significance of the myth and of the attitude of mind of those who recorded the events of the history of Israel in terms of 'salvation-history'. For those who believed, as the prophets of Israel did, that God had really been active from the beginning in the call and subsequent history of their people, the myth was an extension of symbolism. The activity of God in creation, for example, could only be described in symbolic terms, and the traditional myths, borrowed from Meso-potamia, were ready to their hand to supply them with a vocabulary in which to describe the divine activity. The same vocabulary of myth was used to describe what the writers interpreted as divine acts of power, and it was also the only available language in which they could clothe their eschatology, their vision of what the end of history would be like. The dragon, which Yahweh had slain in the beginning to bring order out of chaos, would be slain again by him to restore order in the end.

THE JOSHUA MYTH

The mythical element which had surrounded the figure of Moses had also to some extent included his attendant and successor, Joshua. Thus we find interesting mythical elements connected with the figure of Joshua as the kingly war-leader of Israel as they enter the land of Promise. One of the characteristics of the King-image as we find it delineated in Deut. 17:18–19 is the study of the law, and in the opening verses of the book of Joshua we find that Joshua is enjoined not to let the book of the law depart out of his mouth, but to 'meditate therein day and night', a curious qualification for a war-leader, but a recognized feature of the King-image.²² Then we have an epiphany to Joshua in terms resembling those used to describe the epiphany to Moses at the burning bush. A figure with a drawn sword appears to him, and on being challenged by Joshua announces that he is there as a 'prince' of the Lord's host; he orders Joshua to take his shoes from off his feet for the place whereon he stands is holy ground, using the same words which had been addressed to Moses in Midian (Exod. 3:5). Then comes the account of the capture of Jericho, an episode conceived in wholly mythical terms. Joshua is told to give orders that the host of Israel, preceded by seven priests bearing seven jubilee trumpets of rams' horns and carrying the ark, is to march round the city once a day for six days; on the seventh day they are to do this seven times; then the priests are to sound a long blast on the rams' horns and, at that signal, the people are to give a shout and the wall of Jericho will fall down flat. Joshua carries out these orders and the promised result follows. One of the features of the New Year cult-festival in the autumn was a ritual blowing of trumpets on the first day of the seventh month. It is probable that, in this account of the capture of Jericho, we have another cult myth associated with the feast of the blowing of trumpets. Other early references in the book of Judges suggest that the possession of Jericho, called 'the city of palm-trees', was a matter of some uncertainty (cf. Judges 1:16 and 3:13).

One more striking feature in the Joshua myth calls for notice. In the ninth chapter we have a story of how the inhabitants of Gibeon, by a ruse, induced Joshua to make a peace-treaty with them, and how Joshua, on discovering the fraud, kept the treaty but reduced the Gibeonites to a condition of bondage, evidently an aetiological tale explaining the traditional subservience of the Gibeonites to the

tribe of Ephraim. The story then goes on to relate how five
Canaanite kings attack the Gibeonites who thereupon appeal to Joshua for protection. Joshua's victory over the
five kings is described in mythical terms similar to those
in which the capture of Jericho is described. The rout of
the Canaanite forces is mainly accomplished by a hail-
storm, 'the Lord cast down great stones from heaven upon
them unto Azekah, and they died : they were more which
died with the hailstones than they whom the children of
Israel slew with the sword' (Joshua 10:11). But the completion of the victory is made possible by Joshua's com-
manding the sun to stand still until the enemies are totally
annihilated. We are told in what is a fragment of ancient
Hebrew poetry, that 'the sun stood still, and the moon
stayed, until the nation had avenged themselves of their
enemies.' The compiler records that this stanza is taken
from the book of Jashar, generally understood to be an
ancient collection of Hebrew songs. He ends the story with
the words, 'There was no day like that before it or after it,
that the Lord hearkened unto the voice of a man.' This
episode also has been rationalized in various ways, but it
seems more in keeping with the general tenor of the
Joshua myth to regard it as a fragment of ancient myth
which has been used to glorify the figure of Joshua and to
represent him as possessing powers which not even Moses
had possessed. Although the narrator represents the incident
as unique in the annals of Israel, a similar incident is recorded in the life of the prophet Isaiah. King Hezekiah was
sick, and Isaiah predicted that he would recover and live
another fifteen years; the king asked for a sign that the
prophet's words would be fulfilled, and the prophet offered
him a choice, should the shadow on the dial of Ahaz go
forward or back? The king said that the latter alternative
would be a greater marvel; the narrator accordingly relates

that Isaiah 'cried unto the Lord, and he brought the shadow ten degrees (Hebrew 'steps') backward by which it had gone down on the dial (Hebrew 'steps') of Ahaz' (2 Kings 20:4-11). The author of Ecclesiasticus refers to this incident (Eccles. 48:23), and also alludes to the parallel miracle wrought by Joshua, 'Did not the sun go back by his hand, and did not one day become as two?' (Eccles. 46:4). It is interesting to note a resemblance between the relation of Joshua to Moses, and that of Elisha to his master Elijah. Elisha is represented as receiving a double endowment with his master's powers after Elijah had been taken up to heaven in a chariot of fire, and Joshua does something more wonderful than anything Moses had done.

THE MYTH OF THE ARK

Closely related to the myth of the Shekinah is the myth of the Ark. In the early traditions of Israel the Ark has a double association. One line of tradition connects it with the wilderness wanderings and the early stages of settlement in Canaan; the other line connects it with David and the Jerusalem cult. It is well established that nomad Arab tribes from very early times were in the habit of transporting their tribal gods in a wooden chest in a special tent on camel-back. Hence, during the early period of settlement, when the tribes were moving about independently, as the book of Judges shows to have been the case, each tribe may have had its own sacred chest. The cult myth of the epiphany on Sinai represents the whole of Israel with its twelve tribes as assembled at the foot of Sinai to receive the law and enter into the covenant. But we know that only a comparatively small part of the Hebrew tribes went down into Egypt and experienced the deliverance under Moses;

we also know that the organization of Israel into twelve tribes was not fully achieved until long after the settlement in Canaan, possibly not until the time of Solomon. Hence the tradition which represents the encampment of Israel in the wilderness as a symmetrically arranged square composed of the twelve tribes, with the Ark in its ritual tent at the centre of the square, belongs to the cult myth rather than to history. According to that line of the tradition which connects the Ark with the wilderness journeys, the Ark, borne by the priests, led the march of the twelve tribes and went ahead of them a three days' journey to find out a camping-place for them (Num. 10:33). This procedure continued during the whole of the forty years of the wilderness sojourn, and culminated in the crossing of the Jordan and the capture of Jericho. What reality lies behind the myth is hard to say. In Exod. 33:7 we are told that Moses pitched a tent outside the camp and called it the Tent of Meeting; when he entered into the Tent the pillar of cloud, the Shekinah, descended and stood at the door of the Tent and Yahweh talked with Moses out of the cloud, while all the people watched from their tent-doors. In Deut. 10:1-5 Moses is represented as telling Israel that after the making of the golden calf and the breaking of the first tablets of the law, he was told by Yahweh to fashion a wooden ark or chest in which to put the second tablets. He goes on to say that he did as he was commanded and that the tablets are still in the chest. We, therefore, seem to be dealing with a tradition concerning a tent and an ark very different from the elaborate Tent and Ark of the cult myth. It is to be noted that in the directions for the blessings and cursings at the sanctuary of Shechem, no mention is made of the Ark.

We have only one mention of the Ark in the book of Judges, although it might have been expected that we should hear of the Ark taking part in the various campaigns and struggles in which the tribes were involved during the period of settlement. This reference comes at the end of the book and is at variance with the tradition in Joshua 18 : 1, where the Tent of meeting and, presumably, the Ark, are said to be at Shiloh. In a parenthesis, which is evidently a gloss by the compiler of the book of Judges, it is stated that the 'Ark of the covenant of God' was in Bethel, and that the grandson of Aaron was the priest in charge there (Judges 20 : 27). When the parallel line of tradition, connecting the Ark with David and the kingship, is taken up in the books of Samuel and Kings, we find it in Shiloh, and the myth or legend which now enfolds it was probably preserved in the traditions of that sanctuary.

The first episode is the capture of the Ark by the Philistines. In an engagement between Israel and the Philistines, Israel is defeated. The elders decide to send for the Ark, and it is brought into the camp by the two sons of Eli, Hophni and Phinehas. The Philistines hear of this and are dismayed; they say, 'Who shall deliver us out of the hand of these mighty gods? these are the gods that smote the Egyptians with all manner of plagues in the wilderness.' However, they rally and attack Israel, defeat them with great slaughter, and capture the Ark. They carry it off and deposit it in the temple of Dagon in Ashdod. When the priests enter the temple in the morning they find the image of Dagon fallen upon its face before the Ark. They replace the image upon its base, and the next morning they find it lying broken with its head and its hands lying on the threshold of the temple. Here the narrator remarks that this is the reason why no one ever treads on the threshold of Dagon's temple 'unto this day'. There seems to be a reference to this custom in Zeph. 1 : 9 where Yahweh is represented as saying, 'I will punish all those who leap over the threshold.'

The story goes on to tell how the Ark was carried from one Philistine city to another, and that wherever it went the inhabitants were smitten with plagues like the Egyptians. After seven months of affliction, the priests and diviners advise that the Ark should be sent back to its own country accompanied by trespass-offering. So they put it on a new cart, to which two milch cows are harnessed, and say that if the cows take the cart with the Ark back to its home, they will know that it is the hand of Israel's God that has smitten them; if not, then it has happened by chance. So they shut up the calves and started the cart off on the road to Israel, the lords of the Philistines following to watch what would happen. The cows, lowing for their calves as they went along, took the straight road to Bethshemesh, 'and turned not aside to the right hand or to the left'. The inhabitants of Bethshemesh were in the fields reaping their barley harvest and rejoiced to see the Ark come home. The legend ends on a tragic note. Yahweh is said to have smitten the unfortunate Bethshemeshites with a heavy slaughter because they had looked inside the Ark; the mythical character of the story is shown by the impossible number, 50,070, of the slain. It is clear that the story is a cult myth intended to glorify the God of Israel and to magnify the untouchable sanctity of the Ark.

A similar tendency is seen in the next episode in which the Ark is concerned. A tradition is preserved in Ps. 132 that, during the unsettled years of Saul's reign and the struggle with the Philistines, the Ark had disappeared, and that, when David planned to bring the Ark to his new capital of Jerusalem, a search had to be made for it. This would seem to be the implication of Ps. 132:6, 'Lo, we heard of it in Ephrathah: we found it in the field of Jaar.' Here 'the field of Jaar' is clearly a reference to Kirjath-jearim, the place to which the Ark had been carried after

the disaster at Bethshemesh, and where it had remained forgotten until David, informed perhaps by an oracle, sent to
fetch it. In 2 Sam. 6 we have an account of how David
brought the Ark, on a new cart drawn by oxen, from
Kirjath-jearim, with music and a ritual dance. A disaster
happened, similar to that which had taken place at Bethshemesh. The oxen stumbled, or became restive, perhaps
excited by the music and dancing, and there was a danger
that the Ark might be overturned; one of the men who
accompanied the Ark, Uzza, put out his hand to steady the
Ark, and was immediately stricken dead, to the great alarm
of David and all who were present. David had the Ark taken
into the house of Obed-edom, a man from Gath, and waited
for three months to see if any misfortune befell the family
of the Gittite. As nothing happened, David brought the Ark,
this time safely, to the tent which he had prepared for it
in Jerusalem. Ps. 132 is recognized to be a processional
liturgy, and, while no doubt both incidents have some historical foundation, it is clear that a cult myth has grown
up round the tradition, possibly containing an aetiological
element explaining the sanctity of the sacred stone at Bethshemesh, and the place-name Perez-uzza. It is interesting
to note that the demythologization of the myth of the Ark
is to be found in one of the oracles of the prophet Jeremiah.
In Jer. 3 : 16 we have the announcement, 'In those days saith
the Lord, they shall say no more, The Ark of the covenant
of the Lord; neither shall it come to mind; neither shall
they remember it; neither shall they miss it; neither shall it
be made any more.' The prophet evidently regarded the
Ark as a cult object to which a superstitious reverence had
become attached, and which would cease to have any meaning for those who would receive the fuller knowledge of
Yahweh implied in the terms of the new covenant.

Middle Eastern Mythology

THE ELIJAH AND ELISHA MYTHS

There is no question of the historicity of these two prophetic
figures, but a considerable amount of myth has grown up
round them. During the prosperous period of the Omri
dynasty in the ninth century B.C., Elijah suddenly appears,
without any indication of his background, or of his call to
be a prophet, as the leader of a movement of protest against
the increasing syncretism of Israelite religion. He and his
successor Elisha were behind the revolt of Jehu which
brought about the overthrow of the Omri dynasty. We have
a reference in the books of Kings to prophetic communities known as 'the sons of the prophets' established in the
Jordan valley. Here the traditions relating to Elijah and
Elisha may have been preserved. They bear some resemblance in type to the cult myths which we have been studying. Their purpose is to magnify the power of Yahweh and
his mighty acts performed by the hands of his prophets.

We have first the great scene on Mt Carmel, where Elijah
challenges the priests of the Tyrian Baal, whose cult Jezebel,
Ahab's wife, had introduced into Samaria, to a contest in
order to prove the superiority of Yahweh over the foreign
god. Elijah proposes that each party to the contest shall
erect an altar and lay a sacrifice thereon, and that the god
who is able to send down fire to consume the sacrifice shall
be declared the true god and worthy of Israel's sole worship. The priests of Baal spend all day in frenzied and fruit-
less efforts to induce Baal to bestir himself, while Elijah
mocks them. Then, 'at the time of the evening oblation', an
ancient and wide-spread Semitic custom, Elijah rebuilds the
altar of Yahweh with twelve stones for the twelve tribes of
Israel; he lays the firewood and the pieces of the slain
bullock upon it; he orders those present to pour twelve jars
of water over the sacrifice and in the trench round the altar;

he then invokes Yahweh who sends down fire from heaven consuming the offering, the wood, the stones of the altar, the dust, and even licking up the water that had been poured over everything. The people then acknowledge Yahweh to be God and, at Elijah's command, massacre the four hundred priests of Baal. There is no evidence that Carmel had ever been a place where Yahweh was worshipped, and the various details, such as the twelve stones of the altar and the twelve jars of water, point to the growth of a cult myth round an episode in the life of Elijah which may well have had some basis in reality.

The account of Elijah's flight to Horeb and his experience there is coloured with mythological elements. The forty days of the journey, a common symbolical number, the angelic visitant, and 'the still, small voice' which elsewhere in Hebrew is a phrase used to describe the thin murmur or whisper of a spirit from the underworld (Isa. 29:4; Job 4:16),[23] are all suggestive of the mythological element which has clothed the historical figure of the prophet. Other similar elements appear in the saga. Elijah makes the widow's barrel of meal and her cruse of oil last throughout the three and a half years of the famine, and he restores her dead son to life. The climax of the saga is reached in the account of the prophet's departure from this world. The narrative is a masterpiece of the storyteller's art. Elijah and Elisha start out from Gilgal, and Elijah tries to persuade his servant Elisha to stay behind while he himself goes on by divine command to Bethel. Elisha refuses to leave his master. When they reach Bethel the sons of the prophets, who have a community there, come out to meet them and tell Elisha that Yahweh is going to remove his master from him that day; 'I know it,' he replies. 'Hold ye your peace.' Again Elijah tries to persuade him to stay behind, and again he refuses to be separated from his master. At Jericho the same thing happens, and together they reach the Jordan. Here Elijah wraps his mantle together and smites the Jordan; it divides and they pass over. On the other side Elijah asks Elisha what parting gift he desires from him, and Elisha asks that a double portion of his master's spirit may come upon him. 'Thou hast asked a hard thing', says the prophet, 'nevertheless, if thou see me when I am taken from thee, it shall be so unto thee; but if not, it shall not be so.' Then a chariot (or 'chariots') of fire and horses of fire separate the two, and Elijah is caught up to heaven by a whirlwind. As he ascends his mantle falls and is taken up by Elisha who then returns to the Jordan, smites it with the mantle and, repeating the miracle of Elijah, crosses the river, and begins his own career of prophetic activity. The mythological colouring which had enveloped the tradition of Elijah's activity is heightened in the case of Elisha. He begins by healing a spring at Jericho which produced barrenness; he curses the children of Bethel who had mocked him, and two she-bears come out of the forest and kill forty-two of the children. He multiplies the widow's oil, raises the Shunamite's son from the dead, multiplies loaves to feed unexpected visitors, makes an axe-head float, smites his greedy servant Gehazi with leprosy, and, finally, his sepulchred bones raise a dead man to life (2 Kings 13 : 21). There is one important mythological feature which has become attached to the figure of Elijah and has survived in Jewish belief up to the present time. This is the belief that Elijah would return to earth immediately before the apocalyptic Day of Yahweh to repeat the scene on Carmel and bring about a national repentance. The belief in the return of Elijah was current in the time of Jesus, who interpreted it to his disciples as fulfilled in the ministry and death of John the Baptist. In the Jewish ritual of the Passover at the present day four cups of wine are placed upon the table, each of which has a special symbolic meaning; the third, filled with wine, is known as 'the cup of Elijah', and is left untasted by any one. It is supposed to await the return of Elijah before the coming of the Messiah. An interesting Hasidic legend connected with the cup of Elijah is quoted by Professor Goodenough; [24] a certain Rabbi Mendel was celebrating Passover with a *Marano* in a cave in Spain. A sudden light filled the cave, and the cup of wine which, according to custom, had been left standing upon the table for Elijah, rose high into the air as though someone were putting it to his lips, and then sank back on to the table empty. As the result of this experience Rabbi Mendel taught that Elijah would return as the herald of redemption on the same night in which Israel was liberated from Egypt.

In a niche in Jewish synagogues there stands a chair which is known as 'the throne of Elijah', awaiting his return to occupy it. When a child is brought to the synagogue to be circumcized, he is placed upon this chair while the ceremony is performed.

With the saga of Elijah and Elisha the mythological material of the Old Testament comes to an end. No myths have collected round the figures of the eighth- and seventh-century prophets who live and move in the full light of historical events. There is one exception in the case of Isaiah who is credited, as we have already seen, with having caused the shadow on the dial of Ahaz to go back ten degrees, in order to give a sign to King Hezekiah that he would recover from his sickness. The mythical element reappears in an altered form in late Jewish apocalyptic literature. We have seen that in attempting to give an account of the divine activity in Creation, the Hebrew writers were obliged to fall back on the language of myth, and drew their mythological material largely from the myths of their neighbours, especially from Mesopotamian and Canaanite sources. So when they attempted to describe what they believed would be the shape of things to come, they were again compelled to fall back upon mythological language, now enriched by borrowings from Persian sources, as may be seen from the one completely apocalyptic book of the Old Testament, the book of Daniel.

1. See p. 45.
2. See p. 82.
3. See p. 86.
4. Johnson, A. R., op. cit., p. 81.
5. Kramer, S. N., *From the Tablets of Sumer*, pp. 170 ff.
6. Frazer, J., *Folklore in the Old Testament*, p. 45.
7. Harrison, J., op. cit., p. 142.
8. Thureau-Dangin, F., *Rituels accadiens*, p. 141.
9. Lev. 16 : 15–22.
10. Zech. 13 : 4–6.
11. Judges 4 : 11–17.
12. Smith, S., op. cit., p. 17.
13. Judges 1 : 17–18, 'He was the first among men that are born on earth who learnt writing and knowledge and wisdom.'
14. Smith, S., op. cit., p. 21.
15. Pritchard, J. B., *The Ancient Near Eastern Texts Relating to the Old Testament*, p. 104.
16. Burrows, E., *The Labyrinth*, p. 60.
17. Isa. 1 : 9; 13 : 19; Amos 4 : 11; Jer. 50 : 40.
18. Cook, S. A., *The Religion of Ancient Palestine in the Light of Archaeology*, p. 95.
19. Pedersen, J., *Israel III–IV*, pp. 728 ff.
20. Mowinckel, S., *La Décalogue*, p. 121.
21. Henton Davies, G., 'An Approach to the Problem of Old Testament Mythology' (*Palestine Exploration Quarterly*, 1956), pp. 81–3.
22. Widengren, G., *Sacrales Königtum im A. T. und im Judentum*, p. 30 ff.
23. Hooke, S. H., *The Siege Perilous*, pp. 57–8.
24. Goodenough, E. R., *Jewish Symbols in the Greco-Roman Period*, VI, 2, p. 139; Hooke, S. H., 'The Myth and Ritual Pattern in Jewish and Christian Apocalyptic', *The Labyrinth*, pp. 213 ff.

Chapter 6

MYTHOLOGICAL ELEMENTS IN
JEWISH APOCALYPTIC

THE BOOK OF DANIEL

ALTHOUGH the episodes related in this book are set in the court of Nebuchadnezzar in Babylon at a period after the first captivity of 596 B.C., it is generally recognized today that the book belongs to the period of Antiochus Epiphanes and was written by an unknown author in order to encourage his fellow-countrymen at a time when those Jews who were resisting the Hellenizing policy of Antiochus were undergoing severe trials and persecutions. The book is divided into two parts and is written partly in Hebrew and partly in Aramaic. The first part of the book (Chapters 1–6) consists of a series of episodes in which a young Jew and his three companions resist all attempts to induce them to conform to the heathen religion of their captors, and are delivered by divine intervention out of the most desperate situations.

They demand to be allowed to eat kosher food and refuse the food provided from the royal table. They are vindicated by appearing, after ten days' trial, 'fairer and fatter in flesh' than those who had fed on the heathen food. Daniel's three companions refuse to worship the golden image which the king had commanded all his subjects to worship and are thrown into a fiery furnace. The king sees them standing unharmed in the midst of the fire accompanied by a figure whom the king describes as like 'a son of the gods', and is converted to the worship of the Jewish God. As a punishment for his pride Nebuchadnezzar is turned into a sub-human creature for seven years and eats grass like an ox. When he is restored to his human shape he acknowledges the universal dominion of Israel's God. During Belshazzar's feast, at which the gold and silver vessels of the Temple at Jerusalem, carried off by Nebuchadnezzar, are brought out and used as drinking cups by the assembled guests, a hand appears and writes a mystic inscription upon the walls of the banqueting hall, which none of the king's wise men can read. Daniel is summoned and interprets the inscription; it announces the fall of the Babylonian kingdom and its re-placement by the Medo–Persian power. It is then stated that Belshazzar was slain that night, and that Darius the Mede took the kingdom. It is well known that Cyrus the Persian king captured Babylon without a fight, and that no such person as Darius the Mede is known to history. Finally, the mythical Darius is persuaded by his courtiers to issue a decree announcing that anyone who asked a petition of any god or man except the king for thirty days should be thrown into a den of lions. When Daniel heard of the decree, he went into his chamber where his windows were open towards Jerusalem, and prayed to his God according to his daily custom. He was found by the courtiers in the act, denounced, and duly thrown into the lions' den. In the morning, the king comes to the mouth of the den and 'with a lamentable voice' asks Daniel if his God has been able to deliver him from the lions. Daniel assures him that his God has sent his angel and shut the lions' mouths. Darius has him taken out, and orders all the courtiers who had accused Daniel to be thrown into the den with their wives and children, a macabre touch. Then the king issues a decree that all men throughout his dominion are to worship and fear the God of Daniel.

In these stories, so patently unhistorical, we have a new

use of myth. It is being used as propaganda in a Gentile environment. Yahweh is displayed as Pantocrator, as having universal dominion, raising up and putting down kingdoms at his pleasure, and able to protect his servants under every kind of danger so long as they remain faithful to him. This use of the myth is developed in a somewhat uncontrolled fashion in later Jewish midrashic literature where, for example, Abraham is represented as undergoing similar experiences to those of Daniel and his companions. The same tendency is seen at work in the early Christian apocryphal gospels where both the childhood and passion of Jesus are enveloped in mythological elements.

OTHER APOCALYPTIC USES OF MYTH

But there is another aspect of the use of myth in Jewish apocalyptic which calls for notice. Its beginnings are to be found in such passages as Isa. 27:1 and 51:9–11, where the eschatological activities of Yahweh are described in terms of the ancient myth of the slaying of the chaos dragon. Its development in the book of Daniel and in the extra-canonical book of Jubilees takes the form of the transformation of past and contemporary history into mythological terms. In the second part of Daniel both the empires of the past and the contemporary empire of Greece under Alexander are portrayed as beasts of various kinds, lions, bears, leopards, rams, he-goats, and the final beast is described as a dreadful monster with ten horns, teeth of iron, and nails of brass. He speaks 'great words' against the Most High, oppresses 'the saints of the Most High', that is, the Jewish people, and attempts to change 'the times and the law'. The Jewish people are portrayed as a human figure, 'like a son of man', who comes with the clouds of heaven before the

Ancient of Days and receives the dominion which is to endure for ever. Here the apocalyptic writer sees contemporary history and its consummation in purely mythical terms. The same process can be seen developing in the various Jewish apocalyptic books, Enoch, 2 Baruch, 4 Ezra, and reaches its climax in the great Christian Apocalypse of St John, where all the images of the ancient myth and ritual pattern, the ritual combat, the slaying of the dragon, the sacred marriage, the triumphal procession, and many others, are gathered up into one tremendous description in wholly mythical terms of the winding up of human history.[1]

1. Hooke, S. H., 'The Myth and Ritual Pattern in Jewish and Christian Apocalyptic' (*The Labyrinth*), pp. 213 ff.

Chapter 7

MYTHOLOGICAL ELEMENTS IN THE NEW TESTAMENT

WE have seen that, in the development of the religion of Israel, mythology played an important part. Myths were borrowed from the religions of neighbouring countries and used by Hebrew writers to express in symbolic form their beliefs about the origin of the universe, and above all to present the history of their people as a 'salvation-history', a record of the developing purpose of God who had called Israel to be the vehicle of that redemptive purpose. In the Gospels, the history of Israel reaches its supreme crisis. Certain events took place which brought into existence a new movement of world-wide importance; those who witnessed the events and sought to interpret their meaning, spoke of them as a 'new creation', and described the community which came into existence as the result of these events as a new Israel. They described the central figure of the movement as a second Adam, a new Moses, another Joshua whose name he bore.

We have seen that the mythological elements in the Old Testament gather round certain focal points: the creation of the universe, the fall of man and its consequences, the Exodus from Egypt and the epiphany on Sinai, the challenge of Elijah breaking into the dismal history of the Israelite monarchy, and, finally, the use of myth by Jewish writers to describe how God would wind up world-history. Similarly, when Jewish writers, whose minds had been moulded by these patterns, came to describe what they had been brought to regard as a new and overwhelming display of the might of Israel's God, the God of Abraham, Isaac, and Jacob, seen in a new creation, a new exodus, a new epiphany, a new covenant, and a new future, they used the same mythological patterns to clothe the historical events in which the divine activity was expressed.

The Christ-myth of Drews and Robertson is now little more than a curiosity of literature, but the presence of myth in Christianity continues to agitate the minds of theologians. The demand for a process of 'demythologization' associated with the name of that eminent New Testament scholar Dr Bultmann, has aroused a considerable controversy both in this country and on the continent; but it is very doubtful whether the attempt to purge Christianity of its mythical element can ever be successful. In religion, and above all in that form of it which is Christianity, we are confronted by realities of which it is impossible to speak without using the language of analogy; the mind must have recourse to the help of images and symbols, and of these myth is compounded.

As in the Old Testament the first focal point round which mythological elements gather is the divine act of Creation, the beginning of things, so in the New Testament the first focal point is the beginning of 'new creation', the mystery of the Incarnation.

THE BIRTH NARRATIVES

Of the four canonical gospels only two contain accounts of the birth and childhood of Jesus, namely, Matthew and Luke. There is a wide divergence between their accounts. Luke, in his preface claims to have obtained his information from people who 'from the beginning were eye-witnesses', and his account has far less mythological colouring than that given by Matthew; but the story of the angel Gabriel's appearance to Zacharias in the Temple to announce the birth of John the Baptist, his subsequent appearance to Mary to announce the birth of the Messiah, the angel's announcement to the shepherds of the same birth, and the subsequent chorus of the heavenly host singing 'Glory to God in the highest', are all features of a mythological rather than an historical character. It is also noticeable that here Luke's narrative shows a distinct tendency to be coloured by Old Testament narratives of remarkable births. There are parallels with the story of the announcement of the birth of Isaac to Sarah when she was long past childbearing; also of the announcement of the birth of the hero Samson to Manoah and his wife by an angelic messenger who declares that the child is to be a Nazarite from his birth, and who, after telling Manoah that his name is 'secret', ascends in a flame of fire from the altar. According to the Lukan narrative, the parents of Jesus bring him to be circumcized eight days after his birth; it does not say where the ceremony was performed. Then, after thirty-three days, the regulation period of ritual uncleanness for a woman who has given birth to a male child, the parents go up to Jerusalem for Mary's purification and to present Jesus in the Temple as a first-born child, according to the law. Then they return to Nazareth.

In the Matthaean narrative there is no account of the birth of John the Baptist; Mary is betrothed to Joseph, who discovers, before the time for their marriage arrives, that she is with child. While he is considering putting her away privately, he is told by an angel in a dream that Mary is with child of the Holy Ghost. The angel tells him to take her as his wife, and to call the child Jesus, a name which in Hebrew means 'Saviour', for, says the angel, 'He shall save his people from their sins.' The narrator then adds that all

167

this is happening as the fulfilment of the sign of Immanuel, given to King Ahaz by the prophet Isaiah. To this point we shall return later. Then the narrative goes on to relate that, when Jesus was born in Bethlehem in the time of Herod the Great, wise men (lit. 'mages') came to Jerusalem from the East, inquiring where the King of the Jews had been born, and saying that they had seen his star in the East and had come to worship him. Herod and all Jerusalem are disturbed at the news, and Herod calls the chief priests and scribes together and asks them where the Messiah was to be born. They tell him that, according to the prophecy in Micah 5:2, this would take place in Bethlehem. Herod sends the mages to that village, and, on the basis of their astrological calculations, plans to kill all the children in Bethlehem and the neighbouring district who are under two years old. Joseph is warned in a dream to take Mary and the child and flee into Egypt. The narrator then describes Herod's slaughter of the children and says that this is the fulfilment of a prophecy of Jeremiah (31:15); he also says that the flight into Egypt is a fulfilment of the oracle in Hos. 11:1, 'Out of Egypt have I called my son.' When Herod is dead, Joseph is again told by an angel in a dream that it is safe to return to the land of Israel. He does so, but, discovering that Herod has been succeeded by his son Archelaus, is afraid to return to Bethlehem, and, by angelic direction, goes and settles in Nazareth, in order to fulfil another prophetic word, which has never been identified, 'He shall be called a Nazarene.'

It is generally recognized that the Lukan and Matthaean accounts of the circumstances under which the birth of Jesus took place cannot be harmonized. Luke has invested the historical circumstance with a mythological colouring which is intended to bring into strong relief the divine purpose directing the events, and to show that the pattern of divine activity in redemption, outlined in the Old Testament in those cult myths which we have been studying, has now reached its climax. The canticles which Luke has either composed or borrowed from the psalmody of the early Church are wholly Old Testament in spirit and expression, and are intended to glorify the God of Israel who has thus guided the course of world-history to its consummation. It is noteworthy that in his two chapters devoted to the circumstances attending the birth of Jesus, Luke does not once declare that this or that event was the fulfilment of some particular prophecy; yet he invests his whole narrative in these two chapters with an Old Testament colouring which is the result of a supreme art.

In the corresponding chapters of Matthew, on the other hand, the mythological element is employed in a different way and with a different result. In the first place, we find here the beginning of a tendency which develops to an uncontrolled extent in early patristic literature, the tendency to seek for fulfilment of Old Testament prophecy in events of the life of Jesus. In this short section of the gospel no less than five passages from the Old Testament are cited as fulfilled by incidents in the early life of Jesus. The third of these quotations, from Hos. 11 : 1, in its Old Testament setting runs, 'When Israel was a child then I loved him, and called my son out of Egypt.' Here the prophet is referring to the tradition that the beginning of Yahweh's relations with Israel went back to the deliverance from Egypt. The early Christian writer saw in the word 'son' a reference to Christ, and drew the inference that the new Israel, embodied in Jesus, must have experienced an Exodus from Egypt.

This instance illustrates the second tendency at work in gospel narratives, observable in Luke as well as in Matthew, to find in the life of Jesus a recapitulation of the experience of Israel, as well as that of Moses, since Jesus was for the gospel writers the new Moses as well as the new Israel. The slaughter of the children by Herod and the escape of Jesus and his parents recapitulate the slaughter of the male Hebrew children in Egypt by the Pharaoh and the preservation of Moses. That there was such a conscious or unconscious patterning of the birth narratives in Luke on Old Testament models has been well brought out in a recent article entitled 'St Luke's Genesis', to which reference may be made.[1]

The third tendency at work in the Matthaean birth narrative raises the larger question of the borrowing of mythological material from pagan sources.[2] We have already seen that, in describing the divine activity in Creation the Hebrew writers made use of Sumerian and Babylonian Creation myths, and that in their treatment of such material might be seen the beginnings of a new use of myth as a vehicle of revelation. We have, therefore, a precedent for the use of myth in a way transcending its original function in early religions. The problem meets us in its acutest form in connexion with the Christian dogma of the virgin birth.

It is possible to read the statement in Luke 1 : 35 as implying divine intervention of the same type as is found in the Old Testament accounts of the births of Isaac or of Samson, although the words in Luke 3 : 23, in the genealogy of Jesus, 'being, as was supposed, the son of Joseph', show that Luke himself believed that Jesus had no human father. But the Matthaean statement is unequivocal. Mary is 'found with child of the Holy Ghost'; and the gospel writer goes on to declare that the event is a fulfilment of an oracle of Isaiah which he quotes from the Greek Septuagint version of the Old Testament. This version reads, 'Behold, the virgin shall be with child, and shall bring forth a son, and they shall call his name Immanuel.' Here the point turns on the

Greek word *parthenos*, which is rightly translated 'virgin'. The Hebrew word, however, *'almah*, which the Septuagint translators have rendered *parthenos*, does not mean 'virgin', but 'young woman', that is, any young woman of marriageable age. If the Isaianic oracle be examined in its context, it will be seen that, in a time of trouble and the threat of a foreign invasion, the prophet urged King Ahaz to ask Yahweh for a sign, and when he refused to do so, told him that Yahweh would give him a sign; this was to be the birth of a child to an unnamed young woman; the child was to be named Immanuel, and would grow up to experience the privations which would result from the Assyrian invasion of Judah predicted by the prophet. The primary reference of the sign was to the situation in which it was given. The name given to the child must be considered in connexion with the names given by the prophet to his own children as signs, and its meaning, 'God with us', was intended to tell the king and his panic-stricken people that Israel's God was in command of the situation. If the oracle in Isa. 9:6–7, 'Unto us a child is born', refers to the same child, then the sign of Immanuel would seem to have had a Messianic significance for the prophet, and to have referred to a future Davidic king; but there is no suggestion in the Hebrew text of a miraculous birth from a virgin. Hence the Christian writer's claim that the virgin birth of Jesus is a fulfilment of the Isaianic oracle is based on a mistranslation of the Hebrew. But the fact that Matthew or his source could interpret the oracle in this way shows that the belief in the virgin birth had already taken root in the early Christian community on other grounds. In the first place, it is clear that by the time the canonical gospels were in circulation the divine Sonship of Jesus had been fully recognized, carrying with it the implication of complete sinlessness. On theological grounds the sinlessness of

Jesus was thought to be secured by his conception through the operation of the Holy Spirit without the intervention of a human father, the taint of Adam's sin was therefore not transmitted. This theological argument was later applied to the birth of Mary as being the mother of God, and the dogma of the Immaculate Conception of the Blessed Virgin Mary developed during the Middle Ages until it was established as an article of faith in 1854 by the Papal Bull 'Ineffabilis Deus'. It would seem to have been overlooked that Mary had a human mother, and that the process must go on *ad infinitum*.

In the second place, it has been maintained by many scholars that the current existence of many myths of the divine birth of various heroes of antiquity, such as Herakles, Alexander, and others, played a part in the development of the belief in the virgin birth of Jesus. Whether pagan myths are likely to have influenced Jewish Christian writers may be questioned; but we have seen that Hebrew writers drew on heathen mythology in describing the divine activity in Creation, so that the larger question of the use of myth in describing the divine activity in New Creation cannot be disregarded.

Lastly, a factor in the growth of the cult of the Virgin which must be taken into account is the wide-spread feeling among the uneducated masses for a female object of worship, for a Mother-goddess. This motive was greatly strengthened after the conversion of the Empire to Christianity, bringing into the Church vast numbers of half-educated or wholly illiterate barbarians.

The issues involved in the question of the virgin birth can only be decided on theological grounds, and this is not the place for such a discussion. The main point which we are concerned to stress here is the possibility that we have in the birth narratives of the gospels an extension of the

Mythological Elements in the New Testament

function of myth as a vehicle for conveying truths which lie outside the range of historical evidence.

THE RESURRECTION NARRATIVES

The second focal point round which mythological elements appear to gather is the point of departure of Jesus from the scene of history. In the birth narratives the apocryphal gospels show in an exaggerated form the tendency to use mythological material, so, in a similar way, the resurrection narratives of the apocryphal gospels, as, for instance, the apocryphal gospel of Peter, show the tendency to magnify the mythical element which already appears to some extent in the canonical gospels.

One of the most important elements in the ancient myth and ritual pattern was the myth of the dying and rising god, seen in its earliest form in the Tammuz myth, perpetuated through the ages, and appearing in the various eastern mystery-cults so widely current in the Greco–Roman world in the New Testament period. Some scholars have put forward the view that the gospel narratives of the passion and resurrection of Jesus have been modelled on the pattern of the Babylonian ritual myth, and that, for instance, the ritual humiliation of the king in the Babylonian New Year Festival ritual furnishes the pattern for the account in the canonical gospels of the mock kingship and humiliation of Jesus. This point of view was presented many years ago by the French scholar M. Couchoud in an article in the *Hibbert Journal*. With regard to this, two things may be said. First, if any non-historical factors were at work in shaping the pattern of the passion narratives, they are rather to be looked for in such Old Testament passages as Ps. 22 and Isa. 53, where the sufferings of the godly Israelite, and of the

Servant of Yahweh, are described in terms closely resembling the description of the sufferings of Jesus during his passion. It is one of the generally accepted results of New Testament studies that Jesus regarded the figure of the suffering Servant of Yahweh depicted in the Servant passages of Deutero-Isaiah as the pattern and prefiguration of his own destiny. The story of Philip and the Ethiopian eunuch in the eighth chapter of Acts shows how early this passage was understood by the Church as referring to Jesus. Hence, in the resemblances between the passion narratives and these Old Testament passages, we find, not mythological elaboration, nor the borrowing of a Tammuz myth, but the working of that tendency, to which we have already referred, to find fulfilments of prophecy in the events of the life of Jesus.

Secondly, it may be said that, on a long view, the existence of these ancient myths of a suffering, dying, and rising god, is evidence of a deep-rooted element in religious experience, a sense that something is wrong with the moral order of the universe, and that only the expiatory death of a divine being can meet the situation; and, finally, that in the passion and resurrection of the Son of God the myth finds its realization and justification.

It is mainly in the gospel of Matthew that the mythical elements with which we are concerned appear. There is one detail common to all the synoptic gospels which it is difficult to regard as historical, namely, the statement that at the moment of Jesus's death the veil of the Temple was rent from top to bottom by supernatural agency. Of this incident so eminent a New Testament scholar as Dr C. H. Dodd has said, 'The rending of the veil I take to be purely symbolical.' [3] The three Synoptic gospels also relate that immediately before the death of Jesus there was darkness over the whole land for three hours; Luke adds, according to the best MS. evidence, that the darkness was due to an eclipse of the sun, but, as Origen pointed out long ago, an eclipse of the sun is not possible at full moon. The darkness, like the rending of the veil, is symbolical. In Matthew the mythical element is intensified. In addition to the two incidents already mentioned, he relates that the rocks were rent by an earthquake, the graves were opened, and many bodies of sleeping saints arose and came into 'the holy city' (Jerusalem), and appeared to many 'after his resurrection'. This statement seems to imply that Matthew, or his source, regarded the resurrection of Jesus as taking place immediately after his death, although this is inconsistent with his subsequent narrative. The next mythical element included by Matthew is the story that the priests induced Pilate to place a guard of soldiers at the grave and to seal the stone which closed the mouth of the grave. When the grave was discovered to be empty the Jewish authorities are said to have bribed the soldiers to say that the disciples of Jesus had come and stolen his body while they slept. This curious episode ends with the statement that the soldiers did as they were instructed, and that this belief was current among the Jews at the time when the gospel was written. The story would seem to reflect current controversies at an early period between Jews and Christians concerning the body of Jesus. We have an echo of this in the words attributed to Mary Magdalene in John 20:13, 'They have taken away my Lord, and I know not where they have laid him.'

As is well known, the original form of the gospel of Mark ends abruptly, either intentionally, according to some scholars, or accidentally, according to others, at the eighth verse of Chapter 16 with the words, 'For they were afraid.' The last twelve verses of Chapter 16 are a later addition. All that Mark relates concerning the resurrection of Jesus is that the women came early on the morning of the first day of the week to the grave, and found the stone rolled away and the grave empty. They saw a young man in a white robe sitting by the grave; he told them that Jesus was not there but was risen, and gave them a message to deliver to the disciples to the effect that Jesus would meet them in Galilee as he had told them at the Last Supper. There is no account of any appearances of Jesus, and the mythical element is entirely absent.

In Luke the young man seen by the women has become two men clothed in shining garments whom the women take to be angels. The message given by the young man is considerably modified and the instruction to meet Jesus in Galilee is omitted. The disciples, who are still in Jerusalem, refuse to believe the women's account of what they have seen. Jesus, unrecognized, accompanies two disciples on their way to Emmaus, and reveals himself to them in the breaking of bread. They at once return to Jerusalem to bring the news to the disciples, and find them gathered together debating the report that Jesus was risen and had appeared to Peter, though no account of this appearance is given in any of the gospels. At this point Jesus himself appears in the midst of the assembled disciples and with difficulty persuades them of his reality by partaking of food. Then, according to Luke, on the same evening, Jesus leads the disciples out to Bethany, lifts up his hands to bless them, and in the act of blessing them is parted from them and is carried up into heaven. The words 'and was carried up into heaven' are omitted by some MSS, but the best authorities retain them. Luke has, however, a variant form of the tradition in his second book, the Acts of the Apostles; according to this, Jesus was 'seen' (Gk. *optanomenos*) by the disciples for forty days after his resurrection; at the end of this period, we are told, 'he was taken up and a cloud received him out of their sight' (Acts 1:9), and the context shows that this took place on the Mount of Olives. Ten days then elapse till 'the day of Pentecost was fully come' (Acts 2:1), and we have the account of the descent of the Spirit. The time-table has clearly been adjusted to make the resurrection, ascension, and the descent of the Spirit coincide with the Jewish calendar period of fifty days from Passover to Pentecost. At the moment of the Ascension Luke introduces two men in white garments who tell the disciples that Jesus will return in the same way that they had seen him go into heaven. Here he is evidently offering a parallel to the two men in shining garments whom the women had seen at the grave.

This is the extent to which Luke, or the source, oral or written, which he was using, has invested the resurrection narrative with the element of myth.

Matthew's mythicization has gone much further. According to his account the women do not come to the grave to anoint the body of Jesus, as they do in the other Synoptists, but to watch. They see, descending from heaven, an angel whose appearance is described as like lightning, and his clothing as white as snow; at the sight of him the keepers shake and become like dead men; he removes the stone from the mouth of the grave and sits upon it. He then gives the frightened women a message which is a modified version of the young man's message in Mark. Mark had said that the women fled from the grave in fear, and told nothing to anyone; but Matthew says that they ran from the grave with fear and great joy to bring the news to the disciples. As they went Jesus met them and greeted them. They held him by the feet and worshipped him. He told them not to be afraid, but to tell the disciples to go to Galilee, where they will see him. Matthew ends his account with the statement that the eleven disciples went away to a mountain in Galilee, 'which Jesus had appointed them'. There he came to them; some were doubtful when they saw him; but the rest worshipped him. He told them that all power had been given to him in heaven and on earth, and commissioned them to preach the gospel to all the Gentiles, and to baptize them in the name of the Father, Son, and Holy Spirit.

The Fourth Gospel has no account of the birth of Jesus or his baptism, and the passion and resurrection narratives of that gospel differ in many respects from those in the Synoptic gospels; but the character of the Fourth Gospel raises theological, rather than historical, issues, so that we shall not pursue the question of the Christian use of myth in that gospel. But enough has been said to show that round the two focal points of the entry of Jesus into the world and his departure from it mythical elements tended to gather from a very early date.

To the Hebrew writers who recorded the history of Israel the creation of the universe, the redemption of Israel from Egyptian bondage, and the epiphany of Yahweh on Sinai, were real events which had happened in time, but their character as supreme examples of divine activity placed them beyond the range of ordinary historical narrative. The telling of them became part of an act of worship, a cultic activity, and the language in which they were clothed was such as to magnify the glory of Yahweh, and to remind Israel at the great seasonal festivals of Yahweh's creative and redemptive acts. After the settlement of Israel in Canaan, the myths which related the mighty acts of the gods of the surrounding nations and of the Canaanite deities became part of the early Hebrew traditions, and the Hebrew writers made use of the language of these myths to describe the mighty acts of Yahweh. This has been described as a process of 'demythologization'.[4] But it is better described as the creation of a new relation between myth and reality. We can see myth in the process of acquiring a new function, the function of mediating divine activity to the human mind in terms of analogy and symbol. This process reaches its fullest development at the point when divine activity in redemption reaches its climax in the Incarnation, death, and resurrection of Christ. To say, as we have done, that the gospel writers used the forms and language of myth to describe the events which had taken place before their eyes, is not to deny the reality of these events, but to affirm that they belonged to an order of reality transcending human modes of expression; belonging, indeed, to what Berdiaev has called 'metahistory'. This, of course, is a Christian point of view, and will only be acceptable to those who accept the reality of the Incarnation and its consequences.

1. Goulder, M. D., and Sanderson, M. L., 'St Luke's Genesis' (*Journal of Theological Studies*, April 1957). Also Evans, C. F., 'The Central Section of St Luke's Gospel' (*Studies in the Gospels*, ed. D. E. Nineham).

2. For a full discussion and sources see Meyer, E., *Ursprung und Anfänge des Christentums*, Vol. I, pp. 52 ff.

3. Dodd, C. H., *The Fourth Gospel*, p. 425, n. 1.

4. Childs, Brevard S., *Myth and Reality in the Old Testament*, pp. 95 ff.

Chapter 8

CHRISTIAN MYTH AND RITUAL

THE last aspect of myth which will be considered here is the relation of myth to Christian ritual. Here the wheel has come full circle, and we return to the earliest function of myth, its use as the *muthos*, or spoken part, of the *drōmenon*, the pattern of significant acts which constitute a ritual. A modern scholar has said, 'In Christian ritual and its associated beliefs we are dealing with a living culture fully equipped with an extensive literature, and at the same time having its roots deeply laid in antiquity. Moreover, inasmuch as Christianity was a product of the welter of the religious movements that characterized the Greco-Roman world at the beginning of our era, it gave a new functional significance to the various ancient strands that are embedded in the new culture pattern.' [1]

In the course of the Christian religion as it has developed through the centuries, the focal points of the individual life, the great central moment of national life in the coronation of the sovereign, and, above all, the corporate life of the Church, have all been surrounded with a pattern of ritual consisting of significant acts accompanied by spoken words which are regarded as having power, sacramental efficacy. The spoken part of the ritual is its myth, its *muthos*, and describes a situation in which divine activity is operative to effect the purpose of the ritual. In the Christian rite of baptism certain symbolic acts are performed and certain words are spoken which, for those who regard baptism as a sacrament, have power to bring about a change in the condition of the baptized person, child or adult. For those who undergo the ritual it is a *rite de passage*, a rebirth into a new life, and the myth, the spoken part of the ritual, describes the original situation, the reception of children by Christ, which is reproduced by the words and actions of the priest in the ritual.

In the Christian ritual of marriage, the myth describes the original creation of mankind as male and female, and repeats the divine words which declare that in marriage the man and the woman become 'one flesh' and are indissolubly united. The words and acts of the priest in the ritual have power to bring about the union described in the myth.

The various rituals of ordination of priests and deacons, and of the consecration of bishops, all have this character in common of bringing about through symbolic acts and spoken words a fundamental change in the condition of the persons undergoing these rituals. The coronation of a sovereign has a long and complicated history. Its roots lie far back in the coronation rituals of Egypt and Babylon. A description of the English ritual lies beyond the scope of our study which is concerned primarily with the myth; but a full account of its history has been given by Professor E. O. James in his book *Christian Myth and Ritual*, Chapter 2.

But it is in the great central ritual of the Eucharist that the relation of the myth to the ritual is most clearly seen. Here the function of the myth as the sacred word of power is fully displayed. Like the coronation ritual, the ritual of the Eucharist has a long and complicated history which we shall not attempt to follow here. It has been fully dealt with by the late Dom Gregory Dix in his monumental work *The Shape of the Liturgy*. The first point which concerns us is that the Christian Eucharist is, in its origin, a transformation of the age-long Jewish ritual of the Passover. We have

already seen that the celebration of this annual ritual meal
was accompanied by the recitation of the cult myth of the
Exodus (see p. 144). According to the Synoptic gospels, immediately before his death Jesus celebrated the Passover
with his disciples at Jerusalem. It may be remarked here
that many scholars, following the account in the Gospel of
John, do not regard the Last Supper as a Passover meal; but
recent discoveries relating to the different calendars in use
among the Jews in the time of Jesus have removed the
grounds for this view, and there is no longer any reason to
doubt that Jesus did celebrate the Passover with his disciples.[2]

The accounts of what happened at the Last Supper vary
in details, but common to them all is the central fact that
Jesus, by certain symbolic acts and significant words transformed the Passover ritual into a new thing. He told his
disciples that the Pascal bread which he had blessed and
broken and distributed to be eaten by them was his body,
and that the cup of wine which he had blessed and told
them to drink was his blood. He said that by his death a
new covenant was inaugurated, a new relationship established between God and man. He signified that in what he
was about to do and suffer, the divine activity of redemption prefigured in the ritual and cult myth of the Passover
was now to be fulfilled in him. Whether he intended his
symbolic acts and significant words to become a rite to be
continuously repeated is uncertain; but the Pauline account
of what took place on that Passover night shows that even
before the earliest gospel was written, the primitive Church
had come to regard that as his intention.[3] In the early
Christian treatise known as *The Didaché*,[4] and in Justin
Martyr's *Apology*,[5] we can see the early stages of development of a eucharistic ritual which may be seen in its full
splendour in such a sacramentary as the Sarum Missal

which represents a typical Western Mass as it was celebrated in England during the Middle Ages.

We have seen that in the most important occasion of the Babylonian religious year, the New Year Festival, there was a dramatic re-enactment of the death and resurrection of a god, his triumph over the forces of chaos and darkness, and its result in the subsequent ordering of creation. The ritual was accompanied by the recitation of the *Enuma elish*, a sacred chant which constituted the myth, or spoken description of the situation enacted in the ritual. Other elements forming part of the ritual pattern were a triumphal procession and a sacred marriage. The king played an important part in the ritual, and the renewal of the kingship, upon which the well-being of the community, its salvation, depended, was the central feature of the whole proceeding. We also saw that the spoken part, the myth, was not a mere description of the situation, but had magical power to restore life to the dead god.

We saw that a real situation, the deliverance of Israel from the Egyptian bondage, acquired a cultic significance. It became an annual ritual in which certain symbolic acts were performed and a cult myth was recited which described the original situation, not in historical terms, but in terms calculated to enhance the power and glory of Israel's God and to celebrate his redemptive acts. The death of a victim formed part of the ritual, and the Kingship of Yahweh was reaffirmed in the triumphal song which accompanies the cult myth, 'The Lord shall reign for ever and ever' (Exod. 15 : 18).

Now in the Eucharist we have all these elements centred and transformed in a situation whose ultimate reality transcends the merely historical level. The simple but profoundly significant scene in the upper room in Jerusalem has, in the course of centuries, been expanded and developed into a tremendous dramatic ritual representing in unending repetition the saving mystery of the passion, resurrection, and triumphant vindication of the Suffering Servant who is also the King of Glory.

The details of the ritual and the differences between East and West belong to liturgiology. The point which concerns us here is that into the four-action pattern of the liturgy, repeating the actions of Jesus at the Last Supper, there was introduced at a very early date the myth, the spoken part of the ritual, describing the original situation. The words used are the words in which St Paul described the actions and words of Christ at the Last Supper in his letter to the Corinthian Church. Paul says that he has 'received of the Lord' the account which he here gives of what took place on that occasion. This can hardly mean that he had received the information by a special revelation. It should rather be understood to mean that when he was received into the early Christian community and received instruction as a catechumen, this account of the Lord's actions and words was given to him as an essential part of the sacred tradition of the Church resting upon apostolic testimony.

At the approach to the central point of the canon of the Mass, when the priest, lifting up his hands, utters the *Sursum corda*, he raises the whole pattern of action together with the worshippers to the heavenly sphere, symbolized by the ciborium with the starry canopy. In the myth, the spoken words describing the original scene, the historical event is detached from the stream of history and eternalized. In its place in the ritual it fulfils the true function of the myth; it becomes a word of life-giving power, able, as the priest's words at the moment of communicating indicate, to preserve the body and soul of the communicant unto eternal life.

Here the myth reaches the utmost limit of its meaning

Christian Myth and Ritual

and its function, and our study of its history may fitly have its ending.

1. James, E. O., *Christian Myth and Ritual*, p. vi.
2. Jaubert, A., *La Date de la Cène*, and J. van Goudoever, *Biblical Calendars*.
3. I. Cor. 11 :23–5.
4. *The Didaché*, Chaps. 9 and 10.
5. Justin Martyr, *Apology*, Chaps. 65 and 67.

BIBLIOGRAPHY

BOTTERO, J. *La Religion Babylonienne* (Paris, 1952).

CHILDS, BREVARD S. *Myth and Reality in the Old Testament* (London, 1959).

COOK, S. A. *The Religion of Ancient Palestine in the Second Millennium B.C. in the Light of Archaeology and Inscriptions* (London, 1908).

(*The Didaché*) The Apostolic Fathers I (Loeb Classical Library, 1914).

DRIVER, G. R. *Canaanite Myths and Legends* (Edinburgh, 1956).

ENGNELL, K. I. A. *Studies in Divine Kingship in the Ancient Near East* (Uppsala, 1943).

FRANKFORT, H. *Cylinder Seals* (London, 1939).

FRANKFORT, H. *Kingship and the Gods* (Chicago, 1948).

FRANKFORT, H. *The Intellectual Adventure of Ancient Man* (Chicago, 1946).

FRAZER, J. *Folklore in the Old Testament* (London, 1918).

GASTER, T. H. *Thespis. Ritual, Myth, and Drama in the Ancient Near East* (New York, 1950).

GOODENOUGH, E. R. *Jewish Symbols in the Greco-Roman Period* (New York, 1953 – fol., No. 37 Bollingen Series).

GORDON, C. H. *Ugaritic Literature* (Rome, 1949).

GOUDOEVER, J. VAN. *Biblical Calendars* (Leiden, 1959).

GRAVES, R. *Greek Myths* (2 vols, London, 1955).

GURNEY, O. R. *The Hittites* (London, 1952).

HARRISON, J. E. *Themis. A Study of the Social Origins of Greek Religion* (Cambridge, 1927).

HOOKE, S. H. *The Siege Perilous* (London, 1955).

HOOKE, S. H. (Ed.) *Myth, Ritual, and Kingship* (Oxford, 1958).

HOOKE, S. H. (Ed.) *The Labyrinth* (London, 1935).

HOOKE, S. H. *Alpha and Omega* (London, 1961).

JAMES, E. O. *Christian Myth and Ritual* (London, 1933).

JAUBERT, A. *La Date de la Cène* (Paris, 1957).

JOHNSON, A. R. *Sacral Kingship in Ancient Israel* (Cardiff, 1935).

KING, L. W. *Legends of Babylon and Egypt* (London, 1918).

KRAMER, S. N. *From the Tablets of Sumer* (Colorado, 1956).

MENDELSOHN, J. *Religions of the Ancient Near East* (New York, 1955).

Bibliography

MORET, A. *The Nile and Egyptian Civilization* (trs. M. R. Dobie) (London, 1927).

MOWINCKEL, S. *La Décalogue*, No. 16 Études d'Histoire et de philosopie religieuses (Paris, 1927).

PEDERSEN, J. *Israel: its Life and Culture* (trans. H. Milford) (Copenhagen, 1926, London, 1926).

PRITCHARD, J. B. (Ed.) *The Ancient Near East in Pictures relating to the Old Testament* (Princeton, 1954).

PRITCHARD, J. B. (Ed.) *The Ancient Near Eastern Texts relating to the Old Testament* (Princeton, 1950).

SANDARS, N. K. (Tr.) *The Epic of Gilgamesh* (London, 1960).

SMITH, S. *Early History of Assyria to 1,000 B.C.* (London, 1928).

THUREAU-DANGIN, F. *Rituels accadiens* (Paris, 1921).

WIDENGREN, G. *Sacrales Königtum im Alten Testament und im Judentum* (Stuttgart, 1955).

WITZEL, M. *Tammuz–Liturgien und Verwandtes* (Rome, 1935).

INDEX

Index

Index

Index

Etana, the shepherd, King of Kish, 59; and the eagle, myth of (Sumer.-Bab.), 59–60, 66

Eucharist, Christian, 181–5

Euphrates river, 25, 26, 55, 73, 137

Exile, the, 104, 105, 109

Exodus, Book of, 145, 146, 147, 149, 152, 153

Exodus, cult myth of, 108, 142, 143, 144, 146, 165, 182, 183

Ezekiel, Book of, 41, 95, 113, 132, 146

Ezra, Book of, 118, 120, 164

Feast of Weeks. See Pentecost, Hebrew Festival of

Flood myths. See under Myths

Galilee, 176, 177, 179

Gapn, messenger of Baal (Ugarit.), 84

Geb, earth god (Egypt.), 67, 69, 72

Gehazi, 158

Genesis, Book of, 42, 51, 73, 103, 104, 106–8, 112–13, 130, 133, 136, 139, 140, 142, 146; J-E Version of, 109–17, 118, 119, 121, 129; P Version of, 109, 110, 111, 117–21, 129, 131

Gibeon, 149

Gilgal, 157

Gilgamesh and the Huluppu tree (Akkad.), 55, 59

Gilgamesh, epic of (Sumer.), 17, 32, 36–8, 55, 80, 115; (Akkad.), 36, 37; (Bab.), 49–56; relation of to flood myths, 46–9

Gospels, Apocryphal, 163, 173; Canonical, 165, 166, 171, 173; synoptic, 174, 177, 178, 182

Hadad=Baal as god of thunder and lightning, 81, 86–7

Ham, sons of, 137

Hammurabi, 19; code of, 147

Hannahannas (Hitt.), 101

Hapi=Nile as a god (Egypt.), 77

Hathor, eye of Re (Egypt.), 74, 82, 83

Hattara (Hitt.), 101

Hattusas, Hittite capital, 95

Hauhet, Huh's consort (Egypt.), 72

Hawwah=Eve or Life (Hebrew), 112, 115

Hebat, consort of the storm-god (Hitt.), 97

Hebrew : language; 30, 79; New Year Festival, 120, 121, 125, 149; people, 104, 118, 128, 142, 165; poetry, 30, 48, 80, 82, 83, 84, 94, 106, 107, 121, 128, 133. See also under Israel

Heliopolis, 17, 71

Hercules, 17, 51, 172

Hermopolis, 72

Herod the Great, 168, 170

Hezekiah, king of Judah, 150, 159

Hiribi, god of Sumer (Ugarit.), 93

Hittites, 95–6; New Year Festival of, 98

Horeb, 157

Horus, god (Egypt.), 66, 68, 69, 70, 73, 75, 99

Hosea, 168, 169

Index

Index

Index

Meluhha, Egypt(?) (Sumer.), 26

Memphis (Cairo), 65, 71

Mesopotamia, 11, 18, 19, 116

Methuselah = Methushael or Mathusala, 128

Micah, Book of, 168

Mikku, ritual drum-stick(?) (Bab.), 55–6

Milton, John, 34, 41, 132

Moab, 140

Moses, 14, 128, 136, 142, 145–9, 151, 152, 170

Mot, favourite of El (Ugarit.), 84–6, 93, 106

Mukisanus, Kumarbis's Vizier, 96

Mummu, Apsu's Vizier (Bab.), 43

Mushdamma, great builder of Enlil (Sumer.), 27

Muthos. See Myths, ritual

Myths (definitions and uses); definition as function, 11; distinguished from ritual, 12; diffusion and disintegration of, 16–17; and historical veracity of gospels, 16, 179; as propaganda, 163; as symbolism, 16, 147, 179; as a vehicle of revelation, 171; apotropaic function of, 62, 74, 75, 101

Myths (general):

Akkadian, (Assyro-Babylonian), 32, 36, 38, 56, 65, 86, 96

Assyrian, 19

Babylonian, 14, 15, 19, 38–9, 102, 110, 131, 132, 138, 142, 143

Canaanite (Ugarit.), 14, 15, 79–80, 82, 96, 104, 113, 119, 132, 139, 142; textual sources, 80–1, 92, 94

Egyptian, 32, 65–7, 86, 110, 142

Greek, 34, 87, 93, 102

Hebrew, 58, 92, 104, 147

Hittite, 95, 102

Mesopotamian, 119, 139, 148

Semitic, 34, 46, 58

Sumerian, 19, 32, 34, 36, 38, 45–6, 56, 64, 116, 132, 139

Syrian, 41

Myths (functions, etc.):

AETIOLOGICAL, function of, 13 (Sumer.), 13, 23, 46; (Bab.), 55, 56

BASIC, 19, 22, 23, 39, 41, 46; (Egypt.), 70, 74, 76; (Hebrew), 13, 126, 128, 132, 149, 155

CULT, function of, 13–14; (Ugarit.), 88; (Hebrew), 14, 141–8, 149, 151, 152, 154–7

ESCHATOLOGICAL, function of, 15–16; 108, 140, 148

PRESTIGE, function of, 14–15

RITUAL, function of, 11–13; 14, 22, 46, 49, 56, 89, 92, 100, 116, 120, 123, 128, 141, 143, 173, 180, 184

Myths (subject matter):

CREATION

Assyro-Babylonian, 19, 49

Babylonian, 12, 15, 17, 23, 29, 30, 41–6, 61, 69, 71, 81, 83, 97, 98, 106, 107, 111, 116, 118, 119, 120, 141, 170, 183; origin of the universe, 42–3; organization of the uni-

Index

196

Index

Index

Tiamat, dragon, salt-water ocean, goddess (Bab.), 41, 42, 43, 44, 45, 61, 74, 75, 82, 83, 98, 100, 106, 111, 119, 120, 141, 143

Tigris-Euphrates river valley, 11, 16, 18, 19, 22, 110, 115, 137

Tigris, River, 26, 65, 73

Transfiguration, the, 146

Troy, 15

Tuthmosis III, Pharaoh, 71

Typhon (Egypt.). *See* Seth

Tyre, king-god of, 113

Ubelluris=Atlas (Hitt.), 97

Udom=Edom (?) (Ugarit.), 88

Ugaritic language. *See* Ras Shamra Tablets

Ullikummis, myth of (Hitt.), 96

Underworld: Akkad, 87; Egyptian, 76, 77; Hittite, 100; Semitic, 52–3

Ur, 18, 26, 49, 103

Urshanabi, Utnapishtim's steersman (Bab.), 54

Utnapishtim, ancestor of Gilgamesh (Bab.), 47, 48, 49; =Ziusudra, 53, 114, 130

Uttu, goddess of plants (Sumer.), 33

Utu, sun-god (Sumer.), 21, 25, 31, 34, 37, 38, 114

Uzza, 155

Vegetation-gods, 20, 67

Venus and Adonis, myth of, 41

Vesta, 34

Virgin birth, Christian doctrine of, 170–2

Worm and the toothache, myth of (Bab.), 62–3

Yahweh, 14, 15, 35, 58, 82, 104, 106–8, 110–17, 121, 122–6, 132–3, 139, 142–3, 145–8, 152, 155, 156–7, 163, 169, 170, 178, 183; Apocalyptic Day of, 158; Suffering Servant of, 174, 184

Yahwist writers, 109, 118, 121, 122, 127, 131, 132–3, 135, 137, 138, 140, 142. *See also* Genesis, J–E Version

Yam-Nahar, god of seas and rivers (Ugarit.), 81–2, 83, 84

Yarikh, moon-god (Ugarit.), 86, 93

Yassib, son of Keret (Ugarit.), 89

Yatpan, war-god (Ugarit.), 90

Zab, River, 19

Zacharias, 167

Zaphon, Mt, Baal's Palace (Ugarit.), 82, 83, 85

Zephaniah, Book of, 153

Zeus and Io, myth of, 87

Zion, 15, 146

Ziqqurats, 18, 22, 45, 136, 138

Ziusudra, King of Sippar (Sumer.), 31, 47, 130

Zoroastrianism, 15

Zu, myth of (Bab.), 61–2, 100